ZAPATA: THE IDEOLOGY OF
A PEASANT REVOLUTIONARY

ZAPATA
The Ideology of a Peasant Revolutionary

by ROBERT P. MILLON

INTERNATIONAL PUBLISHERS
New York

Library of Congress Catalog Number: 69-20355
Manufactured in the United States of America

Preface

In contemporary Mexico, Emiliano Zapata and his followers have come to symbolize the essence of the Mexican Revolution of 1910. The focal point of the revolution was the desire for land reform and the *zapatistas,* the men of the South, were the agrarian reformers of the revolution *par excellence.* Zapata issued the Plan of Ayala in 1911 which called for the division of lands and he and his followers fought persistently and courageously for the principles of their plan until the regime of Álvaro Obregón made peace with the remaining *zapatistas* in 1920 by promising genuine agrarian reform. It is principally as a consequence of the struggle of the men of the South that the Mexican Revolution achieved the profound agrarian content which has marked it to this day.

Although the distribution of land was their primary objective, the *zapatistas* also developed an integrated program for national economic, social and political reforms. This national revolutionary program of the men of the South possessed a clearly defined ideological orientation. It shall be the purpose of this work to examine the agrarian heart as well as the broader aspects of Zapata's movement and thereby attempt to clarify the role of the *zapatistas* in the Mexican Revolution. The discussion in the initial chapter of this work concerning the armed struggle of Zapata's movement is not definitive, and will serve merely to make the analysis of *zapatista* ideology more meaningful.

Mexico's intellectual life in the early 20th century was exposed to the varied tendencies of western thought. Liberalism, positivism, Bergsonian intuitionism, anarchism, socialism and many other philosophical currents influenced the Mexican mind. Liberalism had played a significant role in Mexico's intellectual and political history since that nation's independence movement in the early 19th century and formed part of the fabric of Mexican thought. This work will seek to determine the nature of the ideology which Zapata's movement formulated for itself amid this welter of philosophical cross-currents. It will not be concerned with the origins or history of these concepts in themselves.

Mexico, D. F., January 1969 — R.P.M.

Contents

ZAPATA: THE IDEOLOGY OF
A PEASANT REVOLUTIONARY

CHAPTER I

The Struggle Of The *Zapatistas*

*Seek justice from tyrannical governments not
with your hat in your hands but with a rifle in
your fist.* — Emiliano Zapata

Mexico in 1910 was a land dominated by large landed estates
called haciendas. Labor on the hacienda was provided by peasants bound by debt to the estate and by sharecroppers and
renters. Hacienda production tended to be traditional and
routine; owners invested as little capital as possible in their
estates. Production was in part for use and in part for sale upon
the market. That is to say, the needs of the hacienda for such
things as food, building materials, and work animals were met
as far as possible by the hacienda itself. In addition, the hacienda
produced a commercial crop which was sold upon the market.
Part of the proceeds of this sale were used to purchase whatever
essentials could not be produced on the hacienda and the remaining cash income was used by the *hacendado* (hacienda owner)
to maintain himself and his family in customary ease in some
metropolitan center.*

The political, economic and social life of the nation was controlled by an oligarchy composed of the *hacendados,* of members
of the upper echelons of the military, political and religious struc-
tures, and of wealthy merchants and businessmen — all in tacit
league with a small number of foreign capitalists. The vast
majority of the population consisted of peasants bound by debt
to the haciendas.

*The system of production whereby workers are bound to large, pri-
vately-owned, landed estates which produce partially for use and partially for sale upon the market will be referred to in this work as the semi-
feudal mode of production.

The economic and political life of the state of Morelos, the birthplace of Emiliano Zapata and the heartland of his movement, was controlled by a few wealthy men. According to one author,[1] 30 haciendas owned 62 per cent of the total surface area and almost all of the cultivated land in Morelos. Eyler Simpson noted that "of all states in the Republic, Morelos was the prize exhibit of a state in which the villages in their corporate capacity and the inhabitants thereof in their private capacity before 1910 had suffered the greatest losses of land and in which the concentration of landholding in the hands of a few *hacendados* had reached its apogee."[2]

Sugar cultivation and processing was the primary economic activity in the state and most of the inhabitants, although they resided in free villages, worked as laborers on the sugar estates because they lacked sufficient land of their own to cultivate. In contrast to the traditional Mexican hacienda, these sugar estates were operated as capitalist enterprises which sought to maximize profits. In common with the traditional hacienda, however, absentee landlordism was the rule. Large sugar mills with modern machinery dotted Morelos which, in spite of its reduced area, accounted for a third of Mexico's total sugar production. The haciendas constantly encroached upon village lands, not only enlarging their possessions but also depriving small holders of means of support and thereby forcing them to labor for the large estates.

Emiliano Zapata was a mestizo born in Anenecuilco, Morelos, on August 8, 1879.[3] His father owned a small piece of land or *rancho*; the son assisted in the farm chores and attended the local primary school. Emiliano was only 18 when his father died and left him to support his mother and three sisters. (Emiliano's older brother, Eufemio, was married and maintained a separate household.) Emiliano took charge of his father's *rancho* and rented additional land from a neighboring hacienda on which he planted watermelons. He prospered sufficiently to purchase several teams of mules to haul corn for additional income.

Zapata early came into conflict with the system, defending his fellow workers against the haciendas and the local police and *rurales* (rural constabulary). His activities several times forced him to leave the state for his safety and once caused him to be drafted into the army for a short term.

The residents of Anenecuilco elected Zapata president of the village's defense committee in September 1909. In assuming this office, Zapata became the successor of a series of men whom their fellow villagers had elected throughout the centuries to defend the interests of their community. As president, Zapata followed established legal procedures to defend his village's rights before President Porfirio Díaz and before the governor of Morelos, Pablo Escandón. When the village's demands were not met and the neighboring hacienda of *El Hospital* continued to encroach upon Anenecuilco's lands, Zapata led his village on two occasions in 1910 in peaceful occupations and divisions of hacienda lands.

Thus, Zapata was somewhat more independent economically than the peons on the haciendas. Early in life he established himself as a fighter and leader against the status quo.

According to those who knew him personally, Zapata was quite frank, simple and accessible, and possessed great strength of character. Later on he was always considerate with his followers and especially with the peasants, who almost venerated him. He had a great natural talent, learned readily and displayed rapid, almost clairvoyant, insight into people and their problems; it was difficult to deceive him.

In 1910, Francisco Madero, son of a wealthy *hacendado* of the state of Coahuila, initiated the revolution against Porfirio Díaz, the strongman of Mexico since 1876 and the president since 1884. Although Madero's objectives, which were expressed in the formula "effective suffrage and no reelection," were largely political, his revolutionary pronouncement, the "Plan of San Luís" (Potosí), included a provision for the return to small proprietors of lands which had been taken from them illegally. Zapata, attracted especially by this provision of Madero's Plan, immediately enlisted followers and, after contacting Madero through an emissary, initiated the revolution in Morelos. The siege and capture of Cuautla by the *zapatistas* in May 1911 was the decisive victory in the South. Pascual Orozco and Pancho Villa captured Ciudad Juárez in the same month and the Díaz government conceded victory to the revolutionaries. The victories of the *zapatistas* and the possibility that the revolutionaries of the South might attack the poorly defended capital greatly influenced Díaz to take his decision to renounce the presidency. In accordance with the terms of an agreement reached by representatives of Madero and Díaz, known as the Treaties of Ciudad Juárez, Francisco León de la Barra, Mexican ambassador to the United States under Díaz, assumed the interim presidency of the Republic pending general elections.

The *zapatistas* were at first sympathetic toward Madero and tolerated the interim government; they trusted that Madero was sincere in his promises to undertake a program of agrarian reform in Morelos after previous study of the problem and in accordance with legal procedures. Zapata consequently ordered his troops to comply with Madero's request to disband and to disarm. Soon four-fifths of Zapata's forces were disbanded.

The old regime, however, had been defeated in name only. The Díaz bureaucracy and the federal army were intact, and the *hacendados* still dominated the countryside. These elements of the old order proceeded to undermine attempts at reform and to create antagonisms and rifts among the *maderistas*. The federal army provoked bloody conflicts with revolutionary elements in Puebla, León, Tlaxcala, Torreón, Zacatecas and other places but, nevertheless, Madero continued to insist that the revolutionary forces which had brought him victory disarm.

Federal troops, who had been completely driven from Morelos in May, reentered that state and made hostile movements toward the *zapatistas;* consequently, Zapata stopped disbanding his forces. Madero visited Zapata in Cuautla, Morelos, to discuss the problem. At the outset of the discussions, Zapata contemptuously rejected the president-elect's offer to give him an hacienda in the state of Vera Cruz and the right to maintain a small, armed personal escort as the price for his withdrawal from the revolutionary scene. Zapata heatedly explained that he was fighting for the restoration of lands to the peasant villages and was incapable of selling out his followers.

In spite of this bad start, Madero and Zapata finally agreed that the latter would disarm his followers and that, in the measure the *zapatistas* disarmed, the federal troops would withdraw from Morelos. They also agreed upon installing a provisional governor and a military commander in Morelos acceptable to the men of the South. The governor would be authorized to form a commission which would resolve the agrarian problems of Morelos as quickly as possible. Upon hearing of this agreement, León de la Barra, the provisional president of Mexico, ordered General Victoriano Huerta to move against the Liberator Army of the South, as Zapata's forces were called. The *zapatistas*, who had begun to disarm in accordance with the agreement, saw themselves again obliged to retain their arms.

The hostile federal action was taken without the knowledge of Madero. Indeed, Madero's life was endangered because he was still in Cuautla when the threatening federal movements began. Zapata, however, ordered that Madero be allowed to return to Mexico City. Huerta forced an armed conflict upon Zapata's forces at the end of August, and in September the federals launched a general offensive against the *zapatistas*. A personal enemy of Zapata, Ambrosio Figueroa, was named governor of Morelos.

Madero stated publicly in the Capital that the renewal of combat in the South was due to the failure on the part of the government to name Eduardo Hay as governor of Morelos and to the advance of Huerta's forces upon the *zapatistas*. He promised that when he assumed the presidency he would rectify the government's errors and make peace in Morelos on the basis of the agreements of Cuautla. However, Madero did not formally break relations with León de la Barra or Huerta, nor did he insist that the government stop its offensive in Morelos.[4]

The men of the South, confronted with superior forces, resorted to the tactics of guerrilla warfare. Zapata made two attempts to negotiate with the government in spite of the armed conflict which prevailed. When these failed, he led a raid upon the outskirts of Mexico City on October 22-23, 1911, which alarmed the national congress.

Madero assumed the presidency on November 6, 1911. He immediately dispatched Gabriel Robles Domínguez to negotiate with Zapata. The federal troops advanced upon the *zapatistas* while the negotiations were in progress, repeating thereby the tactics they had employed to destroy the peace conferences the previous August.

This time, however, Madero did not even reprimand the federal commanders. Zapata's terms for peace included the withdrawal of federal troops; the formation of a constabulary of 500 *zapatistas* under the command of Raul Madero or Eufemio Zapata or some other acceptable leader to preserve peace in Morelos; the replacement of the governor, and the promulgation of a law of agrarian reform. Although Zapata's conditions were similar to those to which Madero had agreed in Cuautla the previous August, Madero categorically rejected them. He ordered the *zapatistas* to surrender immediately and unconditionally, in which case he would pardon them.[5] He instructed Robles Domínguez to inform Zapata that "his attitude of rebellion is damaging my government a great deal and that I am not able to tolerate its continuation for any reason.[6]

Zapata's answer was to continue his struggle and to proclaim the Plan of Ayala on November 28, 1911. It remained the banner of the men of the South throughout the revolution.

The federal general, Juvencio Robles, devastated Morelos in a cruel campaign. His excesses led Madero to replace him by General Felipe Ángeles (later a prominent follower of Francisco Villa) and the fighting subsided somewhat.

Stanley Ross, a student of Madero and his epoch, arrives at the conclusion in regard to the break between Madero and Zapata that "if Zapata's basic demands had been met, it is reasonably certain that the Morelos insurgents would have submitted to the government." Charles Cumberland, author of another major study on the Madero era, reaches a similar conclusion. Both authors place the responsibility for the conflict between the federal government and the *zapatistas* upon the maneuverings of reactionaries and counterrevolutionaries.[7]

The break between Madero and Zapata indeed was inevitable, considering that Madero conceived the revolution in almost purely political terms and retained intact the bureaucracy and army inherited from the Díaz regime. As we have seen, Madero had called for at least partial measures of land reform in his Plan of San Luís. He claimed, however, that the Treaties of Ciudad Juárez by which his victory over Díaz was confirmed prevented him from fulfilling this provision of his Plan because these treaties obliged him to accept the legality of the court judgements and administrative acts of the previous Díaz administration.[8] The latter had succeeded in tying Madero's hands before relinquishing power.

Madero stated he wished to promote the formation—at a moderate pace—of small private properties in rural Mexico and to return *ejidos* (communal lands) to villages. He formed two commissions to study the problem of agrarian reform, the National Agrarian Commission and the Executive Agrarian Commission. The latter commission issued a report in April 1912 which stated that the purchase by the government of lands from large estates and the division of national lands was an unsatisfactory and impractical way to carry out an agrarian reform, and recommended the return of *ejidos* to the villages. The government, however, did little to implement the recommendation of the commission, limiting itself to recovering *ejido* lands which could be proven to have been illegally alienated from the villages. In addition, the government bought some lands from large landowners and surveyed and recovered some national lands which, in turn, were divided among small holders. These activities, however, barely scratched the surface of the agrarian problem.[9]

Madero summed up his attitude toward land reform when he declared in June 1912 that "it is one thing to create small properties by means of constant efforts and another to divide the large properties, which I have never thought of doing, nor offered to do in any of my speeches or proclamations."[10]

In December 1912, Luís Cabrera, speaking in the Chamber of Deputies in support of his project for the return of *ejidos* to villages by expropriating the lands of neighboring haciendas, stated that the chief executive was hostile to his project. According to Cabrera, Madero wished to establish the peace before undertaking economic reforms, whereas Cabrera claimed that it was precisely the implementation of these reforms which would provide a solid basis for establishing and maintaining the peace.[11] Madero, however, refused to see the light.

Madero's ideal of establishing a regime of political democracy in Mexico was impossible to realize while the economic and social organization of the nation remained semi-feudal in character. Likewise, it was impossible to carry out an agrarian reform "in accordance with the law and on the basis of previous study" while the Díaz bureaucracy and army remained intact and the *hacendados* retained control of their estates.

The conservatives succeeded in provoking an armed conflict between the federal government and the Liberator Army of the South before Madero assumed the presidency. Once president, Madero played into the hands of those who wished to conserve the old order when he failed to come to terms with the *zapatistas* and other revolutionary elements. That he failed to do so indicated Madero's essential conservatism in respect to economic and social reforms. His primary goal was political reform, but he failed to comprehend that political reforms could be implemented only if accompanied by profound changes in the nation's social structure.

Madero's shortsightedness was probably a consequence of his social class background — he belonged to one of the wealthiest landowning families in Mexico — which blinded him to the necessity for thoroughgoing reforms, since these would undermine the power and privileges of the class into which he was born. Political reforms, on the other hand, would give members of his class a more equal opportunity to influence the conduct of government. Some individuals in history have succeeded in overcoming their class background; Madero was unable to do so. He opposed some aspects of the old order but at the same time was unable to identify himself completely with the forces for social revolution. As a consequence, Madero was crushed between the opposing forces for conservation of the old order and for social revolution.

Huerta put an end to the inept Madero government by a military coup in February 1913, and instituted a dictatorship in support of the old order. While the coup was in process, Zapata offered Madero 1,000 men to combat the rebellious federal soldiers garrisoned in Mexico City; Madero did not accept the offer.[12] Also, when General Felipe Ángeles returned to Mexico City with some of his troops to assist Madero in putting down the revolt, Zapata agreed not to attack either Ángeles's troop train or the virtually undefended Cuernavaca. Rosa King, an observant British woman resident in Cuernavaca at the time of these events, has noted that "I know now that when Madero waited in prison only one military man in Mexico was preparing to lead his troops to the rescue — and that was, of all men, Zapata, whom he had treated badly."[13]

Shortly before he was assassinated on Huerta's orders, Madero told his fellow prisoner, General Ángeles, that Zapata had been right in distrusting the federal officers and in predicting their defection when the two had met in August 1911. At the same time, Madero told another fellow prisoner of Huerta, Federico González Garza: "As a politician I have committed two grave errors which have caused my downfall: to have tried to content everyone and not to have known to trust my true friends. Ah! If I had but listened to my true friends, our fate would have been different; but I paid more attention to those who had no sympathy for the revolution and today we are experiencing the consequences."[14]

Huerta at first attempted to negotiate with Zapata, but the lines were too clearly drawn between the *hacendado*-government elements and the peon revolutionary groups for him to be successful. And Zapata, personally, could not be bought off. Zapata's replies to Huerta's overtures were eloquent in their revolutionary spirit. For example, Zapata declared to Huerta: "We do not want the peace of slaves nor the peace of the grave.... We want peace based on liberty, on the political and agrarian reform promised by our political creed; we are incapable of trafficking with the blood of our brothers and we do not want the bones of our victims to serve us as a staircase to public offices, prebends or canonships."[15]

The intransigence of the *zapatistas* forced Huerta to commit a considerable number of troops to the campaign in the South, thereby frustrating his plans to crush the revolution in the North before it could get organized. Huerta returned to the old policy of devastation in Morelos, with Robles in charge again. The bulk of the *zapatista* forces were driven from Morelos in the latter part of 1913, but they continued to be active in neighboring states. Zapata himself operated in Guerrero where his forces occupied the major towns and laid siege to Chilpancingo, the state capital, which fell on March 24, 1914. In April 1914 the *zapatista* forces returned to Morelos and by the end of May had taken all the towns in that state except the capital, Cuernavaca. It was placed under siege in June and taken in August 1914.

Meanwhile, the Constitutionalists, nominally under the leadership of Venustiano Carranza, advanced on the capital from the North. Pancho Villa's Division of the North bore the brunt of the fighting; it broke the back of the federal army in the battles of Torreón. San Pedro de las Colonias, and Zacatecas. Threatened from north and south, Huerta fled the country in July 1914.

The revolution was not immediately victorious, however, for a rift had opened between the Villa and Carranza factions of the Constitutionalists. The *zapatistas* represented a third force, although they tended to be friendly toward the *villistas*.

The men of the South mistrusted the *carrancistas* and especially Carranza himself. The sources of this mistrust were many. Carranza had never clearly defined his position on political, social and agrarian reforms and he had assumed the executive power of the nation without consulting the will of other revolutionary chieftains in the country. The Constitutionalist army under the command of General Álvaro Obregón occupied Mexico City in August 1914 without first coming to an understanding with the Army of the South. Before entering the capital, Obregón negotiated with the federal commanders the Treaties of Teoloyucan, under the terms of which Constitutionalist troops substituted federal troops in outposts facing the Army of the South. The fourth clause of the second treaty of Teoloyucan reads: "Federal troops garrisoned in the towns of San Angel, Tlalpan, Xochimilco and others facing the *zapatistas* will be disarmed in the places which they occupy as soon as the Constitutionalist forces relieve them."[16]

When the Constitutionalists moved into the federal positions, clashes began with the *zapatista* forces. As shall be noted later, a more radical group within the Constitutionalist movement wished to implement social reforms, including land reform, similar in content to those advocated by the *zapatistas*. Nevertheless, it was the moderates under Carranza's leadership who dominated the Constitutionalists and gave that movement its political orientation.

Carranza apparently was willing to take some measures of agrarian reform; however he did not contemplate implementing such an immediate and thoroughgoing reform as the men of the South wished. In a speech delivered in Hermosillo, Sonora, on September 24, 1913,[17] Carranza made a brief reference to land reform without, however, entering into details on the reforms he proposed to implement. In the summer of 1914, the governor and military commander of Nuevo León, Antonio I. Villarreal, isued a decree, with Carranza's consent, which suppressed debt-peonage in his State.[18]

Similarly during the months of August and September 1914, various Constitutionalist governors and generals decreed the abolition of debt-peonage in the states of Puebla, Tlaxcala, Tabasco and San Luís Potosí. In Aguascalientes, the governor decreed one day of rest in the week and an eight-hour day for labor. In Tabasco, the governor provided for a minimum wage and the eight-hour day. The governor of San Luís Potosí, in addition to suppressing debt-peonage, decreed the abolition of the *tiendas de raya* (estate or "company" stores), established the eight-hour day and a minimum wage, and created a labor department to help resolve the problems of rural and urban workers.[19] On August 6, 1914, the Sub-Secretary of the Interior (*Gobernación*) ordered the Constitutionalist governors in the various states to organize councils and committees to gather information on the agrarian problem. The governors were to send the information collected to the Secretariat of Development (*Fomento*) in order that the "First Chief" (Carranza) could use the information to resolve the agrarian problem.[20]

On many occasions, however, Carranza had manifested hostility toward measures of immediate and thoroughgoing land reform. He had ordered Villa in 1913 (according to the account of Villa's chief of staff, Colonel Manuel Medina) not only to desist from dividing lands among the peasants, but also to return to their original owners those already partitioned in Chihuahua during the governorship of Abraham González. Carranza adopted a similar attitude in respect to the division of lands which General Lucio Blanco had initiated in the region of Matamoros, Tamaulipas.[21]

Villa's and Carranza's representatives, meeting in Torreón in the summer of 1914, had reached an agreement to end the dispute between the two leaders. Carranza, however, rejected the eighth clause of the agreement on the grounds that "the matters treated in it are alien to the incident which motivated the conferences." The clause which Carranza found unacceptable stated that the revolutionary conflict was "a struggle of the disinherited against the abuses of the powerful," noted that

Mexico's misfortunes were due to praetorianism, plutocracy and clericalism, and promised to continue fighting until the federal army was destroyed and replaced by the Constitutionalist army. The clause went on to promise that the Constitutionalists would install a democratic regime in Mexico, "procure the well-being of the workers," "emancipate the peasants economically" by distributing lands equitably "or by other means which tend to resolve the agrarian problem," and "punish and demand responsible conduct from members of the Catholic clergy who supported Victoriano Huerta either intellectually or materially."[22]

Felix F. Palavicini, close collaborator of Carranza and Secretary of Public Instruction and Fine Arts in the latter's cabinet from 1914 to 1916, indicated the true stature of his mentor when he declared in a book on Carranza which he edited in 1916: "Carranza's subtlety and virtue in politics have not permitted him to flatter low passions among the rabble. He never has offered a socialist program, he has not promised an inconsiderate division of lands, he has not asserted the absolute domination of the labor unions, he has not offered the spoliation of the wealth of others for impatient glutonnies and he has maintained himself within the limits of reality, without offering more than he can fulfill and fulfilling always, infallibly, what he offers."[23]

As for the possibility of cooperating with the *zapatistas,* Carranza had expressed his intransigent attitude toward the revolutionaries of the South shortly after initiating his armed movement. In the spring of 1913, Dr. Francisco Vázquez Gómez tried to induce Carranza to unite his forces with those of other revolutionaries, including the *zapatistas.* Vázquez Gómez, a medical doctor, had served as Minister of Public Education during the interim presidency of León de la Barra. His brother Emilio had served in the same cabinet as Secretary of the Interior, but had resigned in protest over the rightist policies of that regime. Both brothers, sons of poor peasant parents from Tula, Tamaulipas, favored a thoroughgoing land reform in Mexico and sympathized with the *zapatistas.*

In anticipation of his meeting with Vázquez Gómez, Carranza declared in a letter dated May 14, 1913, to Roberto V. Pesqueira, confidential agent of the Constitutionalist government in Washington, that "Doctor Vázquez Gómez will arrive here this afternoon. Don't be concerned; in case I accept his services it will be only because he adheres to our cause and without any compromises on my part respecting his brother and his followers, because I am resolved not to let anyone join with us who does not follow our ideas and our ends, as I manifested to you when you were here."[24]

After his interview with Vázquez Gómez, Carranza wrote again to his confidential agent in Washington on May 18, 1913. Carranza said he rejected Dr. Vázquez Gómez's suggestion that all revolutionaries unite under a single program and demanded as the price for cooperation between the Constitutionalists and the *vazquistas* the "unconditional adhesion" of the latter to the Plan of Guadalupe.* Carranza asserted he made it clear to Vázquez Gómez that the Constitutionalists would make no compromises in return for support from the *vazquistas*.[25]

General Alfredo Breceda, Carranza's private secretary at the time of the interview, has made his chief's attitude even clearer. In a work which he published later, Breceda declared that Vázquez Gómez's proposals, which he judged were intended to unite the *carrancistas* "in abominable union with the rabble of Zapata," were "absurd." He added that Carranza announced to the press at the time that he would never accept alliances with elements which were not "strictly clean and honest."

Finally, Carranza made perfectly clear his unwillingness to cooperate with other revolutionaries except on his own terms in a letter to Dr. Vázquez Gómez, dated May 30, 1913. Carranza, in part, declared: "I am sorry to differ with the ideas which

*Carranza's political plan issued in March 1913. It called for the overthrow of Huerta and the restoration of constitutional government in Mexico and it designated Carranza as "First Chief of the Constitutionalist Army in charge of the Executive Power."

you express to me concerning the union of the revolutionary parties in our Republic, but since completely noxious elements figure in some of them, they would not offer any guarantee for the consolidation of peace in our country, but rather, far from it, they would bring the germ of new revolutions. Therefore, I consider that the only elements acceptable are those which adhere unconditionally to the Plan of Guadalupe, without any compromise on the part of the Constitutionalist movement which I head."[26]

Representatives of Zapata had six interviews with Carranza shortly after the Constitutionalists occupied the capital; the first two interviews were held in Tlalnepantla and the others in the National Palace. Carranza's attitude was hostile. He refused to accept the Plan of Ayala, claimed that it was illegal to partition lands and declared he had 60,000 rifles with which to subject the *zapatistas*. During the fourth interview, he denied the *zapatistas* permission to enter Mexico City because, he claimed, they were bandits and lacked a banner. Before they could enter the capital the men of the South must submit themselves unconditionally to his government and accept the Plan of Guadalupe. He went on to counsel Zapata's representatives to abandon their leader, to forget about land reform and to join the Constitutionalist army, receiving in return promotions to the next higher rank. In the last interview Carranza declared land reform illegal and demanded, as the condition for peace, the unconditional submission of the *zapatistas* to the Constitutionalists.

Respecting the Plan of Ayala, Carranza maintained according to the account of one of the *zapatistas* present, that "he was not disposed to recognize anything enunciated in the Plan of Ayala for the Constitutionalist army had fought for another Plan, that of Guadalupe; ... that he considered the land revolution illegal because it was unquestionable that if a landlord or another person was stripped of properties which he had acquired—no matter how, so long as legally—he would have to protest and with the protest would come another armed struggle." He went on to say that "I cannot recognize what you have offered because the *hacendados* have rights sanctioned in law and it is not possible to take their properties from them and give them to those who have no right to them." Finally, he exclaimed: "The notion of dividing lands is preposterous. Tell me what haciendas you have, as your property, which you can divide, because one divides one's own, not another's."[27]

In the latter part of August 1914, Carranza sent "unofficial" representatives to Cuernavaca to parley with representatives of the revolution in the South. The *zapatistas,* who by now thoroughly distrusted Carranza's motives, insisted adamantly, as conditions for coming to terms, that the *carrancistas* accept the social and political principles of the Plan of Ayala—land reform and the designation of an interim president by a convention of revolutionary chieftains. In a letter to his "unofficial" negotiators, Carranza offered to accept the agrarian demands of the Plan of Ayala on condition that the *zapatistas* join the Constitutionalist army and submit themselves to Carranza's authority. The *zapatistas,* of course, felt they could not surrender to a man who had been a governor and senator under Díaz, whose revolutionary plan claimed for him the right to exercize the executive authority of the nation, and who never had stated clearly the social reforms which he intended to put into practice. Zapata would have betrayed his followers if he had delivered into Carranza's hands the cause for which his people had fought for so long and with so much bloodshed merely on the promise of the latter to carry out agrarian reforms. Huerta had made similar promises. The parleys ended in deadlock.*[28]

A convention of revolutionary chieftains and their representatives was held at Aguascalientes to resolve the impasse between the revolutionary factions. The principal business of the Aguascalientes Convention was to settle the rift between the Villa and Carranza factions of the Constitutionalists, but the Convention nevertheless promptly voted to invite Zapata to send

---

*See the Appendix for a discussion of various interpretations of the bases for the conflict between the *zapatistas* and *carranistas.*

representatives. Zapata sent a delegation of 26 members headed by Paulino Martínez and Antonio Díaz Soto y Gama. Villa had a large representation but Carranza's delegates were in the majority at the frequently unruly meetings.

The *villistas* immediately announced their complete support for the Plan of Ayala, and the Convention voted to accept the Plan "in principle." In addition, the Convention assumed national sovereignty,[29] accepted an apparent offer by Carranza to resign his position as "First Chief of the Constitutionalist Army and in charge of the Executive Power," and elected Eulalio Gutiérrez interim president of the nation.

Carranza, however, refused to accept the dispositions of the Convention, claiming that he had merely stated that he was "disposed to resign," but that the Aguascalientes Convention lacked the authority to accept his resignation or to depose him. The *carrancista* delegates did an about face and supported their chief. Then the Constitutionalists retreated from Mexico City to Vera Cruz, where they promptly issued decrees on land reform in order to reinforce their revolutionary following. Villa's and Zapata's forces jointly occupied the capital.[30]

Frictions soon developed between the *villistas* and *zapatistas,* although the formal relations between the two revolutionary forces remained good. Villa began to take arbitrary actions which did little to cement relationships between his followers and the men of the South. When the first elements of the Liberator Army of the South had entered the capital in November 1914, two *zapatista* intellectuals, Octavio Paz and Conrado Díaz Soto y Gama, began to publish a revolutionary newspaper entitled *El Nacional* on the press of the former newspaper, *El Imparcial.* Only five numbers were issued, however, because when Villa entered the capital early in December he ordered all presses closed for five or six days. Afterwards, according to Octavio Paz, Villa gave the press on which *El Nacional* was printed to certain private individuals "who had intrigued greatly to obtain it." In addition, Villa initiated a series of reprisals against his personal enemies, which included revolutionaries who had criticized him as well as counterrevolutionaries. In this fashion, Villa ordered the assassination of Paulino Martínez, one of the most prominent intellectuals associated with the *zapatistas,* because Martínez had dared criticize him publicly in the past.[31]

The convention, reduced to its *villista* and *zapatista* representatives, moved to Mexico City where it organized a government with ministries of Public Instruction, Commerce, Treasury, War, Interior, Agriculture, and Justice. The last two ministries went to *zapatistas.* The delegates began a series of debates on a program of revolutionary reforms in which the more conservative views of the men of the North frequently clashed with the more radical concepts of the men of the South. The program of reforms was not completed until the spring of 1916, by which time the Convention was thoroughly dominated by the men of the South.

Neither the *villistas* nor the *zapatistas* submitted themselves completely to the authority of the Convention government. The Convention's authority was weakened by the conflicts of interests within it and, especially, by conflicts between Zapata's representatives and the *villistas* in charge of the executive authority of the Convention, General Eulalio Gutiérrez and later General Roque González Garza. Furthermore, in practice, the exigencies of constant warfare made for military dictatorships under Zapata on the one hand, and Villa on the other.[32]

Effective military cooperation between the Division of the North and the Liberator Army of the South, which had always been extremely limited, ceased shortly after it began, Villa remaining supreme in the North and Zapata dominating the South. The *zapatistas* took Puebla and Villa attempted to mop up *carrancista* elements which threatened his supply lines from their positions in Jalisco, Michoacán, Tamaulipas and Sonora. The Constitutionalist army in Vera Cruz, under the command of Obregón, armed and provisioned itself well, and early in January 1915 retook Puebla from the poorly equipped *za-*

patista defenders and on January 28 entered Mexico City.[33] Obregón withdrew his forces from the strategically unimportant capital in March, and in April shattered Villa's forces in the famous two battles of Celaya. Subsequently, the *villistas* suffered one defeat after another until by the late summer of 1915 their area of effective operation was reduced to Chihuahua and Durango. The *villistas* never again possessed national military potential.

Much of southern Mexico was under the control of the Army of the South, and Mexico City changed hands several times between the *zapatistas* and *carrancistas*. When the men of the South evacuated the capital for the last time in August 1915, the Convention government withdrew with them, establishing itself first in Toluca and then in Cuernavaca. Later when the Convention withdrew from Toluca, many of the *villista* members tried to journey north to join Villa but were largely dispersed by *carrancista* forces. The Convention government in Cuernavaca, nevertheless, still included a few *villista* delegates from the northern and central states.

Carranza clearly indicated his attitude toward the *zapatistas* in a speech delivered in Querétaro on January 2, 1916. Carranza's words revealed the contempt of the bourgeois for the peasant and of the head of an organized army for the guerrilla. "The military struggle is now almost ended. The most important forces of the Reaction have been defeated and dispersed in the North, and there remains only that which is not Reaction, which is not anything: *zapatismo,* composed of hordes of bandits, of men without consciences who cannot defeat our forces because they are a nullity as soldiers and who know only how to blow-up undefended trains, ... but who will have to disappear when the Constitutionalist Army very soon begins to concern itself with them."[34]

In the spring of 1916, Carranza sent General Pablo González into Morelos with 40,000 soldiers organized into six columns. Although the rapacious general gained many initial victories and captured the principal towns in Morelos and neighboring states, his forces were discouraged by persistent *zapatista* attacks and by the scourges of malaria and dysentary. The *zapatistas* recaptured some of the major towns of Morelos from the *carrancistas* in December 1916 and January 1917, including Jojutla, Yautepec and Cuautla. González retreated to the federal district in February 1917, leaving Morelos, the greater part of Guerrero and parts of Puebla in the hands of the men of the South.

How were the *zapatistas,* standing alone, able to defeat a well-equipped army? A word of explanation is in order concerning the nature of Zapata's forces and the character of the struggle in which they engaged for so many years.

Zapata's army was unlike the other major armies of the revolution, which had access to financial resources and to international supplies of arms and munitions which the *zapatistas* lacked. Suffering a chronic shortage of military equipment, especially of the two essentials of the contemporary warfare — artillery and machine guns — the *zapatistas* adopted the tactics of guerrilla warfare, at which they became expert. They organized themselves into bands, which in turn could be marshalled rapidly into larger forces for major engagements, varying in size from a few dozen to several hundred members, each with its own leader who in turn was subject to Zapata's authority. The peasant communities supplied both men and sustenance to these bands. In turn, the Army of the South established the procedure of alternating its soldiers between three-month periods of active service and of agricultural labors in their villages. The *zapatistas,* in short, were a people in arms.

Zapata attempted to organize his forces efficiently, as is evident from his decree of January 31, 1917 which provided for the reorganization of the army on the basis of infantry, cavalry and artillery units with supporting engineering, military sanitation, justice and administrative services. In spite of Zapata's efforts, his forces never attained the discipline and organization of a regular army nor, apparently, of a modern guerrilla force such as that which operates in South Vietnam in the 1960's. Thus, for example, we have the testimony of *zapatista* veteran Octavio Paz who mentions an attack upon Puebla in May 1916, which not only failed but resulted also in the death of one of the attacking generals because various *zapatista* forces failed to arrive in time for the battle due to a "misinterpretation of the hour" of attack.[35]

In spite of their shortcomings in organization, Zapata's men nevertheless were quite effective fighters. They laid traps and ambushes, cut supply lines, took small towns by storm, destroyed the smaller enemy units and harassed his larger forces. They were expert at capturing the elements of war from the enemy and, in addition, fabricated explosives and cartridges on their own. True to the tenets of guerrilla warfare, they avoided formal battles with major enemy forces until they were fairly certain of victory, thereby denying the enemy the opportunity to destroy them as an effective military force at one blow (as Obregón did the *villistas*). As their strength grew, the men of the South besieged and took major towns, such as Cuautla, Cuernavaca and Puebla and, as we have seen, they occupied Mexico City on several occasions. After its final retreat from the capital in 1915, the Army of the South reverted to the guerrilla warfare tactics which it had employed so successfully in the past.[36]

Octavio Paz has given a vivid account of the effectiveness of Zapata's tactics in his struggle against Pablo González's army in 1916-17. According to Paz, Zapata maintained only a few small forces with him at general headquarters which could be sent speedily into action at any place, at any time. The individual guerrilla units, meanwhile, kept in constant movement, attacking the *carrancistas* not only within Morelos, but also in the states of Mexico, Puebla, Tlaxcala, Oaxaca and Hidalgo.

These tactics completely disconcerted the enemy who could never put his fire power into effective use. If the enemy advanced with a large force, he never found anyone to fight; if he divided his forces, he exposed them to destruction in ambushes and assaults. The *carrancistas* had against them "not only armed men who knew the terrain, but the terrain itself, which was suitable for ambushes, as well as the climate and the inhabitants in general." Guerrilla warfare and malaria soon decimated the "resplendent army" of Pablo González.[37] Baltasar Dromundo aptly summarized the results of this *carrancista* campaign. "More than 8,000 malarial soldiers, more than 5,000 dead and as many more wounded and mutilated, a return home of wretches and men undone; this is the result of the campaign in Morelos which weakened the *gonzalistas* in spite of the war material which Carranza received."[38]

The prominent *carrancista*, Luís Cabrera, speaking in the national congress in 1917, recognized the effectiveness of Zapata's methods of warfare when he claimed that, although it was easy to defeat the *zapatistas* politically and economically, it was indeed quite difficult to conquer them militarily.[39]

The various forces engaged in the Mexican Revolution, including the Army of the South, frequently committed excesses. However, the forces which combatted the *zapatistas,* from those of Díaz to those of Madero (with the exception of General Ángeles's command), Huerta and Carranza were especially cruel and vicious in their campaigns. The torture, mutilation and assassination of unarmed peasants as well as of prisoners of war, the rape of peasant women, the sacking of towns, the burning of villages, the deporting of inhabitants of Morelos to other parts of the republic, and the destruction of crops, animals and implements of work were commonplace occurences. We even have the case of the *maderista* general, Juvencio Robles, who, in imitation of General Weyler's procedure during Cuba's struggle for independence, attempted to "reconcentrate" the villagers of Morelos into the larger towns. Crimes of Nazi proportions were perpetrated against the *zapatistas.* For example, in June and August 1916, *carrancista* troops killed 466 men, women and children in Tlaltizapán, Morelos, where Zapata maintained his general headquarters. The Mexican writer, Alfonso Taracena, claims in his study of Zapata's movement that "the *carrancistas* burned, robbed and killed with more ferocity than that displayed by the *huertistas* in their work of desolation and extermination against the *zapatistas*." The *carrancistas* under Pablo González were guilty even of dismantling the sugar mills and selling the machinery, along with railroad rails and engines, as scrap-iron in the capital.[40]

In respect to the latter depredations, we again have the testimony of Alfonso Taracena, among others, who states that when the *carrancista* soldiers withdrew from Morelos in February 1917, they carried with them as booty to be sold in Mexico City such things as household furniture, doors and windows; machineery and other articles of iron and bronze from the sugar mills; church bells; and "even the lead piping of the sewers."[41]

Former *zapatista* general Gildardo Magaña enters into this matter in greater detail. He notes that sugar production — the principal economic activity of Morelos — diminished from 1911 onwards until it virtually ceased due to the vicisitudes of warfare. The *zapatistas,* continues Magaña, "carried off horses, arms and objects easy to transport" from the haciendas, but they did not harm the machinery of the sugar mills, "which could have been used with but few repairs" when the armed conflict ended. However, Magaña explains, the forces under the command of Pablo González completely plundered the haciendas of Morelos in 1918 and 1919, destroying the buildings and carrying the mill machinery to Mexico City to sell as scrap iron. In their campaign, the *carrancistas* "used the most reprehensible procedures, and not only on the haciendas but also in the cities and towns, carried out the most unbridled rapine in the memory of the state, to the point of overshadowing the nefarious labor of the *huertista* general, Juvencio Robles." The *zapatistas,* of course, were blamed for this destruction but, since it was impossible to charge them with carrying off the machinery, "silence was guarded on this fact." Many persons believed the *carrancista* tales, concludes Magaña, because they did not know the true state of affairs in Morelos and, furthermore, because the "mercenary press' had predisposed them against the men of the South.[42]

Although they did not match their adversaries, Zapata's followers nevertheless were at times guilty of murder and pillage. The division of the Army of the South into bands which frequently operaed on a semi-independent basis increased the problem of discipline. Some of the *zapatista* chieftains had reputations for cruelty, and a few even fought among themselves. Zapata's associate, Antonio Díaz Soto y Gama, readily admits these facts, but claims that Zapata did all in his power to control excesses and punished leaders guilty of crimes.[43]

Octavio Paz, another of the intellectuals associated with the men of the South, has claimed that although Zapata had a kindly heart and generally pardoned mistakes, he was inflexible with traitors and with those who committed crimes against peaceful villagers. Zapata realized that the peasant villages were the principal support of the armed movement and that they might well turn against the revolution if it abused them. Zapata, says Paz, always brought the accused to trial before a special military tribune when he was at his general headquarters in Tlaltizapán.[44]

Zapata gave numerous evidences of his desire to prevent excesses by his followers. Thus, he told Otilio Montaño on April 30, 1911, that he wanted the support of intellectuals "so that they may put order into these people for whom, once the fight begins, there is no God who can hold them back."[45]

In several of his military circulars Zapata showed his concern to prevent abuses by his followers. In July 1913 he issued instructions to his officers which said, in part: "You will endeavor at all costs to maintain good order among the troops, especially when they enter the villages, giving every guarantee to the lives and interests of the inhabitants, improving the behavior of the soldiers as much as possible."

Zapata issued an extensive order on October 4, 1913, in which he commanded his armed followers to respect the lives and properties of others: "Under no pretext nor for any personal cause should crimes be committed against lives and properties." The order prohibited pillaging, robbery, or "any other kind of depredation" when a town or other center of population was taken, "no matter what its importance." Those in command were charged with the responsibility to prevent such abuses and to punish infractors "energetically" with the objective of "suppressing those acts which are contrary to our creed and to the cause which we defend."

The document went on to order the revolutionary chieftains to punish civilians who took advantage of disorders and combats to steal or commit other depredations and to warn these leaders that they would be held responsible for depredations which occurred in villages taken by revolutionary forces in the zones under their command. The order concluded with an exhortation to the revolutionary chiefs to preserve the greatest possible discipline and order among the troops because "the constant practice of order and justice will make us strong" and "the Revolution and the motherland will esteem their worthy sons who make our creed the verdict of equity and justice, our efforts the tomb of tyrants, and the triumph of our ideals the prosperity and well-being of the Republic."[46]

A circular May 31, 1916, authorized villagers to organize and to arm themselves in defense against "evildoers and bad revolutionaries."[47]

After the men of the South forced Pablo González's army to withdraw from Morelos, Zapata appointed General Prudencio Casals "Inspector General of the entire zone governed by revolutionary troops," with authority to judge summarily and execute all individuals caught committing robbery, armed assault, or rape by violence.[48] These and other measures were necessary in order to suppress the vagabondage and brigandage which had arisen as a consequence of the disorganization and misery which the *carrancista* terror had wrought in Morelos.

Fighting did not cease in the South with the retreat of Pablo González's army early in 1917; the *carrancistas* made a number of raids into Morelos in 1917 and 1918, killing peasants, burning crops and driving off cattle. Hunger and misery spread in Morelos as a consequence of these depredations. Many starved to death and others in their weakened condition were easy victims of an epidemic of "Spanish influenza" which assaulted the state in 1918. Demoralization spread among Zapata's followers and some desertions occurred. Four *carrancista* columns attacked Morelos in August 1918, and in December General Pablo González led some 40,000 men into that state; a number of *zapatistas* surrendered as the enemy advanced. According to Octavio Magaña, former general in the Army of the South, by 1919 only 10,000 *zapatista* soldiers remained of the some 70,000 who had withdrawn from Mexico City in 1915.[49] Nevertheless, the revolutionaries of the South were still able to give worthy combat to the federal forces.

Zapata's concern over the dwindling of his forces led him to fall into a trap which the *carrancista* colonel, Jesús M. Guajardo, carefully laid for him. The latter offered to join his forces with those of Zapata, and when Zapata rode into the hacienda of Chinameca to accept the transfer, he was shot down. Many Mexicans recall the date of Zapata's death, April 10, 1919.

Many of Zapata's followers either surrendered or retired from the struggle after their leader's death, but a nucleus led by Generals Genovevo de la O and Everardo González continued the struggle. These remaining *zapatistas* made their peace with Obregón after the latter overthrew Carranza in 1920.

The United States played a significant role in the Mexican Revolution.* American investments in Mexico had grown considerably during the era of Porfirio Díaz, and by 1910 totalled more than a billion dollars. They were especially heavy in the oil and mining industries and in agricultural and pastoral activities. Great Britain also had extensive investments in petroleum and mining, as well as in public utilities and agriculture. French capital was important in the textile industry and Spaniards had extensive holdings in textiles, retail trade, and agricultural lands.

*Since it would require another study of book length to arrive at a substantial and documented interpretation of that role, I will limit myself here to a few remarks which I hope will give perspective to the anti-imperialist posture of the *zapatistas,* to be discussed later.

The American government used various means to protect the interests of its citizens in Mexico and to influence the course of events in the revolution. It used its power of diplomatic recognition to strengthen or weaken governments in power; it controlled the shipment of U.S. arms and munitions so as to favor one or another of the contending factions; it threatened armed intervention; and it actually did intervene in Mexico with its armed forces on two occasions. Henry Lane Wilson, the U.S. ambassador to Mexico, played a prominent role in the coup which brought Huerta to power and led to the assassination of Madero, although the U.S. government subsequently set about to undermine the Huerta regime. Initially hostile to the Carranza regime, the American government nevertheless extended diplomatic recognition to it in October 1915, thereby strengthening the authority of Carranza's government, which was still engaged in a struggle with the *zapatistas*.

American armed forces occupied Vera Cruz in 1914, ostensibly to prevent the Huerta regime from receiving a shipment of arms through that port. Troops under the command of General John J. Pershing were sent into northern Mexico in 1916-1917, on the pretext of punishing Villa and his men for their raid upon Columbus, New Mexico. Many Mexicans felt that an ulterior motive of these interventions was to warn revolutionaries of possible dire consequences if they should dare threaten the interests of American investors in Mexico. The manifest willingness of the U.S. government to employ its tremendous power to defend what it considered its interests in Mexico would seemingly have undermined the support of the more radical factions of the revolution, since these factions were more likely to take direct actions against American property interests in Mexico and thereby bring the wrath of American imperialism down upon that nation.[50]

CHAPTER II

Agrarianism

The land free, the land free for all, land without overseers and without masters, is the war-cry of the Revolution. — Emiliano Zapata

The men of the South manifested their agrariansim in virtually all of their activities and pronouncements. Indeed, the struggle for land reform was the heart of Zapata's movement. Since we shall rely considerably upon the revolutionary programs and manifestos of the *zapatistas* in this and the following chapter in order to determine the ideals and objectives of that movement, the question arises as to the reliability of these documents as genuine indicators of the motives of the southern revolutionaries. The discussion to follow will mention some efforts by the men of the South to implement their ideals — surely the best test of sincerity of purpose. It is worth noting here, nevertheless, that contemporary Mexican public opinion in general as well as many historical investigators conceive Emiliano Zapata to be the epitome of the genuine social revolutionary.[1] Zapata, however, does have his critics, many of whom wrote during the revolution proper when the upper classes were anathematizing Zapata and his supporters.[2]

Zapata and his followers took up arms in 1910 to achieve agrarian reform and steadfastly upheld their demands for the distribution of lands upon the interim government of León de la Barra and the regime of Madero. In a famous interview held in Mexico City in 1911, Madero made the mistake of offering Zapata a *rancho* for his services. Zapata declared he was not fighting for personal gain but for genuine agrarian reform and concluded by remarking: "The only thing we want, Mr. Maʻero, is that the lands be returned to us which were stolen by the *cientifícos* hacendados.*"[3]

Zapata and Otilio Montaño, a schoolteacher turned revolutionist, formulated the Plan of Ayala in November 1911. Zapata dictated the Plan and Montaño wrote and polished it, although the two discussed it thoroughly in the process.[4]

The initial articles of the Plan disavowed Madero's leadership of the revolution on the grounds that he had betrayed the principles of his Plan of San Luís. Madero, charged the Plan of Ayala, had allowed the greater part of the elements of the old order to retain their positions of power and influence, while he had countenanced the persecution, jailing and killing of genuine revolutionaries. The document went on to pledge support for the Plan of San Luís. Article III recognized General Pascual Orozco as "Chief of the Revolution"; if he refused to accept this recognition, it would be accorded to Zapata.

Articles VI, VII, and VIII are the heart of the document. They provided three bases for land reform: (1) Land usurped in the past from its rightful owners was to be restored; the armed villagers were authorized to take immediate possession of these lands. (2) One-third of the lands of the haciendas were to be expropriated by reason of public utility and with prior indemnification in order to provide *ejidos* (communal lands), *colonias* (colonies) and *fundos legales* (private rural properties) for those who did not receive sufficient lands under the first provision. (3) Finally, any *hacendados, científicos* or *caciques* (local political bosses) who opposed the Plan would have all their property nationalized without indemnification.

The most important of the remaining articles indicated the manner in which the democratic political life of the nation was to be restored once the revolution was victorious. Article XII stipulated that upon the victory of the revolution a convention of the principal revolutionary chieftains of the nation would

*Wealthy and influential supporters of the Díaz dictatorship.

name an interim president of the republic who in turn would call general elections. Article XIII proposed a similar procedure in regard to the formation of the state governments: the principal revolutionary leaders of each state would designate the provisional governor of the state, who in turn would convoke general elections.[5]

The Plan was thus essentially agrarian in nature although it upheld the almost purely political Plan of San Luís and it stipulated, in order to avoid the imposition of mandates upon the Mexican people, the manner in which the state governors and and the national president were to be designated upon the victory of the revolution. (This aspect of the Plan will be examined in greater detail in the next chapter.) Under the terms of the Plan lands could be granted to individuals or to communities. No provision was made for the organization of agricultural cooperatives (although they were not forbidden either) similar, say, to the communal *ejidos* organized during the regime of Lázaro Cárdenas in the 1930s.

The Plan of Ayala was revised twice. In the revisions, Zapata was designated "Chief of the Revolution" in view of the fact that Pascual Orozco had betrayed the revolutionary cause by siding with Huerta, the need for genuine agrarian reform was reemphasized, and the supporters of the Plan pledged to continue their struggle until Huerta was overthrown and all reactionaries removed from positions of power and a government established which put the agrarian reform into practice.[6]

The Plan of Ayala was the banner of the *zapatistas* throughout the revolution. Zapata and his men were intransigent in their insistence that the revolution accept the agrarian and political provisions of the Plan; it was their price for peace in Mexico.

There is overwhelming additional evidence that agrarianism was the heart of Zapata's movement. Thus, in his negotiations, mentioned previously, with the León de la Barra and Madero regimes, Zapata stressed above all the need for agrarian reform. His demands for the appointment of a governor acceptable to his movement and for the removal of federal troops were intended to prevent the possibility of federal treachery and to ensure the implementation of land reform in Morelos. In short, political reform was necessary to insure agrarian reform. Zapata summed up the two basic principles of the Revolution as "political reform and agrarian reform which can give the well-being and the peace which is desired."

With victory over Huerta near, Zapata issued a "Manifesto to the Nation" on October 20, 1913. It is an eloquent revolutionary document which, as shall be demonstrated later, conceived the revolution in much broader terms than did the Plan of Ayala. Nevertheless, the manifesto did not suggest any changes or additions to the Plan.

The *zapatistas* proclaimed an "Act of Ratification of the Plan of Ayala" in June 1914. Although it contained considerations of a political character, the need for land reform was the essential theme of the act. The act reaffirmed the principles of the Plan of Ayala and declared that the agrarian parts of that Plan must be raised "to the range of constitutional precepts."

After many difficulties had arisen in attempts to reach an accord with Carranza, Zapata issued a manifesto "To the Mexican People" in August 1914. It is a brilliant and fervid statement of social revolutionary principles. It stressed that the revolution—contrary to Carranza's conception in the Plan of Guadalupe—was not fought alone for political aims or for a change in governmental personnel. The conquest of traditional liberal objectives such as freedom of the press, effective suffrage, and democratic judicial reform, were also declared inadequate goals. Only the complete destruction of the old order and creation of a new on the basis of a thorough redistribution of land would suffice to terminate the revolution. "The country wants something more [than political changes and "timid reforms"], it wants to break once and for all with the feudal era, which by now is an anachronism; it wants to destroy with one blow the relations of master and servant and of overseer and slave, which are the only ones that reign, as regards farming, from Tamaulipas to Chiapas and from Sonora to Yucatán." Again, no specific proposals beyond the Plan of Ayala were made.

Zapata issued a decree on September 8, 1914, which implemented the agrarian provisions of the Plan of Ayala. The decree nationalized the properties of the enemies of the revolution and stipulated that funds derived from the sale of urban properties were to be used to form "banking institutions dedicated to fomenting agriculture" and to pay pensions to widows and orphans of revolutionaries. The nationalized forests, lands and waters were to be "distributed in common among the villages that so solicit and divided into lots among those who so desire." The distributed land could not "be sold or alienated in any form; all contracts or transactions which tend to alienate these possessions being null." These rural properties could change hands only "by legitimate transmission from fathers to sons."[7]

In stipulating that urban as well as rural properties were subject to expropriation, the decree made the terms of the Plan of Ayala more precise, since the Plan referred only rather vaguely to enemy properties (bienes) in general. The decree went beyond the Plan in providing that funds derived from the sale of these urban properties would be used in part to found agricultural credit banks, since the Plan had stipulated only that funds derived from the sale of enemy properties would be used to pay war indemnities and to provide pensions for widows and orphans.

The decree also would seem to indicate that Zapata had discarded the idea of paying indemnities for expropriated lands. The Plan provided for the restitution of lands to villages and individuals and for the nationalization of the properties of the enemies of the Plan without indemnification, but it stipulated that indemnities must be paid for the one-third of the lands of large estates which were declared subject to expropriation by reason of public utility. The decree seemed to indicate that Zapata intended to push the agrarian reform on the basis of

nationalization of enemy properties rather than the expropriation of lands by reason of public utility and thereby avoid
the problem of indemnities. Most large landowners, of course,
were enemies of the Plan of Ayala.

Zapata's letter on September 4, 1914, to Antenor Sala,
wealthy sympathizer of the *zapatistas,* confirms our supposi-
tion.[8] In this letter, Zapata rejected the idea that indemnities
should be paid for lands which were expropriated. It would be
impractical, according to Zapata, to pay indemnities because of
the large sums of money involved and also it would be unjust
to the peasants since the land was theirs by right. In addition,
the state would have to burden the labor of the poor in order to
acquire the funds to pay the indemnities. Zapata went on to
note that the Plan of Ayala contained three principles of agrarian
reform: restitution of lands to villages and individuals, expropriation by reason of public utility, and confiscation of enemy
goods, and "in order to put these three great principles into practice money is not necessary, but rather honesty and will power
on the part of those charged with carrying out these principles."
In this statement, Zapata apparently did not consider it necessary
to pay indemnities even for land expropriated by reason of public utility. Finally, I may note that the *zapatistas* did not in
fact pay indemnities for the lands they expropriated and distributed among villages and individuals. They demonstrated thereby the depth of their revolutionary convictions because it would
have been virtually impossible to implement a thoroughgoing
program of agrarian reform if indemnities had to be paid former
owners.

In the debates in the Aguascalientes Convention the delegation from the South urged the Convention to proclaim its sovereignty, to accept the Plan of Ayala, to remove Carranza and to
elect a provisional president to head a provisional government.
In letters to his delegates, Zapata adamantly insisted that the
Convention accept these objectives. After much debating in
which the *villistas* were generally pro and the *carrancistas*

con, the Convention accepted the Plan of Ayala "in principle."[9]
No further revolutionary program was adopted by the Convention at this time.

The *zapatistas* continued to uphold their agrarian ideals during the period of the Constitutionalist government headed by Carranza.[10] The men of the South may be said to have indirectly influenced the incorporation of social reforms in the Constitution of 1917, even though only *carrancista* delegates attended the Constituent Convention of 1916-1917. The basic necessity for agrarian reform which the *zapatistas* demonstrated *par excellence* forced the conservative members of the Convention (including Carranza) to acquiesce in the constitutionalizing of social reform.[11] Indeed, the Constitution incorporated some of the most vital features of *zapatismo*.

Zapata issued a manifesto on April 20, 1917, which again emphasized that the objective of his movement was to break the monopoly of land in the hands of the few. This monopoly, according to the manifest, "denied even the right to live" to the Mexican people and condemned them to subsist as slaves in their own nation. The struggle, therefore, was directed solely against the monopolizers of land who exploited human labor and produced nothing but misery and hunger. "To fulfill the Plan of Ayala is our sole and great commitment; therein will lie all our intransigence. In everything else, our policy will be one of tolerance and attraction, of concord and of respect for all freedoms."[12]

In another manifesto, issued on May 20, 1917, Zapata again emphasized that the achievement of land reform was the principal objective of the Liberator Army of the South. After claiming that the Constitutionalist regime deceived no one any longer and that everyone now recognized Carranza as a traitor to the revolution, the manifesto went on to clarify the nature of the revolution.

"The revolution which that army [the Liberator Army of the South] heads has been fighting for seven years now to obtain

that which the powerful and the deceivers have bound themselves
not to concede: the liberation of the land and the emancipation
of the peasant.

"THE LAND FREE, THE LAND FREE FOR ALL,
LAND WITHOUT OVERSEERS AND WITHOUT MAS-
TERS, such is the war-cry of a revolution which is directed
against the *hacendado*, that obstructive remnant from other
epochs; but this cry is respectful of all rights which do not signi-
fy a usurpation, a monopoly or a spoliation."[13]

Without providing further examples, the following quotation
will sum up the essence of Zapata's agrarianism. In a letter dated
March 31, 1913, he declared:

"I recommend to you that you please express to your brother
the lawyer Emilio Vázquez Gómez, that my soldiers and I
long for peace, but we wish that this peace be in accord with the
principles which we sustain and that, if it is not in this form, we
will continue fighting for our demands until we conquer or suc-
cumb; that if he has determined to enter into agreement with
the present government, that in his conscience he will find the
result of his work, but I will continue fighting and I will not depart
the slightest from the precepts of the Plan of Ayala."[14]

The Convention government, under the influence of the
zapatistas, issued an Agrarian Law[15] on October 26, 1915, which
provided for the implementation of the provisions of the Plan
of Ayala. The Law provided for the restoration to communities
and individuals of all lands which had been illegally taken from
them and authorized the nationalization of the goods and properties of the enemies of the revolution. It announced, "for the
effect of creating small properties," the expropriation by reason of
public utility of all lands which exceeded in area certain stipulated
limits. In order to establish the maximum legal area of land which
individuals could possess, the lands of the nation were classified
into 18 categories according to their quality and humidness
and to prevailing climatic conditions as well as, in some cases,
to the use to which they were put (pasture, henequen, rubber).
The maximum areas permissible under the Law varied from 100

hectares in irrigated lands of prime quality located in hot climates to 1,500 hectares in unimproved lands located in certain arid areas of northern Mexico.

The Law went on to stipulate, among other things, that lands expropriated by reason of public utility were to be distributed among individuals in lots which would be of adequate size to maintain a family. Indemnities would be paid for lands expropriated, "taking as a base the fiscal census of 1914"; lands ceded to individuals and communities could not be alienated. Beneficiaries must work their lands personally and they would be deprived of their lands if they left them uncultivated for two consecutive years. The proprietors of lots could organize cooperative societies to exploit their lands or to sell their products in common. The nation's waters and forests were nationalized and villages were authorized to exploit the forests under their jurisdiction, employing "the communal system" for this end. The Ministry of Agriculture and Colonization was authorized to create regional agricultural and forestry schools and to establish experimental stations. The Law concluded by ordering the municipal authorities of the nation to implement this law "without loss of time and without any excuses or pretexts whatsoever" and under penalty of severe punishment as "enemies of the Revolution" if they were "remiss or negligent" in so doing. Agricultural commissions designated by the Ministry of Agriculture and Colonization would later review and rectify where necessary the dispositions of the municipalities.

The Sovereign Revolutionary Convention government (the government established by the Aguascalientes Convention in 1914 and which by this time was dominated by the *zapatistas*) issued a Regulatory Law on the National Agrarian Question[16] at the same time that it issued its Program of Politico-Social Reforms in Cuernavaca on April 18, 1916. The preamble set the profoundly revolutionary tone of this law. It declared that the "supreme end of the Revolution is the division of lands among the peasants," that the peasants "right away and by force of arms should and can recover the properties which were taken from them in the epoch of the dictatorship"; that the government would intervene only in order to legalize the peasants' actions, to issue definitive property titles and to settle boundary disputes between villages; and that the federal government alone was competent to carry out the agrarian reform in a uniform and just manner since the state governments were subject to the influences and manipulations of the wealthy and powerful individuals of the region.

The law authorized villages which had not yet done so in accordance with the provisions of the Plan of Ayala to enter immediately into possession of lands, forests and waters which had been alienated from them in the past "without it being necessary to wait for the authorities to give them what legitimately belongs to them." The national government was given exclusive jurisdiction over agrarian matters and was to carry on its agrarian functions through the Ministry of Agriculture. The latter was to send commissions to the different parts of the republic to legalize and make effective the distribution of lands; these commissions were to inform themselves thoroughly in each locality and were to avoid the slightest favoritism in their labors. The Minister of Agriculture was to decide cases of dispute which might arise between the villages and the agrarian commissions; the villages could appeal the Minister's decision to the Sovereign Revolutionary Convention, whose judgement would be final. This latter recourse was to exist only until special land courts were established in accordance with the Plan of Ayala. The state governors were to facilitate the work of the Ministry of Agriculture and were to obey the resolutions of the latter "without objections or pretexts." The Ministry of Agriculture was to be "responsible before the nation for the frauds, abuses and omissions which are committed in the distribution of lands carried out under its directions." The Minister of Agriculture was liable to from two to ten years imprisonment for malfeasance in office and, in addition, to the confiscation of all his belongings if he was found guilty of subornation or bribery.

The law thus consciously avoided the shortcomings in terms of revolutionary efficacy of Carranza's well known law of January 6, 1915, which, shortcomings and all, was incorporated into Article 27 of the Constitution of 1917. Carranza's law made agrarian reform depend upon the prior fulfillment of complex legal procedures, while Zapata's law authorized the peasants to distribute lands among themselves immediately; the government was to legalize the peasants' actions later. The law of January 6 placed the implementation of the agrarian reform in the hands of the state governors, whereas the law of April 16 consciously avoided this pitfall, giving the national government exclusive jurisdiction over agrarian matters. The *zapatista* initiative, in short, was thoroughly revolutionary; the *carrancista* law contained shortcomings which permitted counterrevolutionary elements to delay and frustrate the agrarian reform.

It is true that the Carranza law provided for the granting of lands to villages which could not acquire sufficient lands for their needs under the provision for the restitution of alienated lands. The *zapatista* measure, however, was intended merely to implement article six of the Plan of Ayala which provided for the restoration of lands to villages; the Plan of Ayala in addition provided for the expropriation of one-third of the hacienda lands and the nationalization of the properties of the enemies of the revolution. The Constitutionalist law limited the properties affectable to those immediately adjacent to the villages concerned; the Conventionalist measure placed no such limitations on the affectability of lands. Also, if applied with truly revolutionary spirit—as the men of the South were sure to do—either the provision for the restitution of lands or for the nationalization of enemy properties was adequate to carry out a thoroughgoing land reform in Mexico.

The Ministry of Agriculture and Colonization of the Convention government issued a pamphlet in 1917, "The Fractioning of the *Ejidos*,"[17] which clarified the *zapatista* concepts on land tenure. The pamphlet criticized the traditional form of tenure in the *ejidos* in which a "keeper of the lands" (*guardatierras*) redistributed the parcels among the members of the community every year. This method was inefficient, according to the pamphlet, because it restrained the incentive of the agriculturalist to improve his parcel by works of drainage, irrigation, and deforestation, since the following year his lot would be given to someone else who either would benefit undeservedly from the labor of its former possessor or would allow the improvements to go to waste. Hence, few improvements were made and the villages continued to live on the verge of misery. In order to avoid these difficulties it was necessary to divide the *ejidos* into lots of sufficient size to maintain a family; the proprietor would have to cultivate his lot and could not alienate it in any form. The edict went on to note immediately that this system of tenure was not ideal. "No one pretends that this system of property is perfect. The inconveniences to which it is subject are perfectly known in as much as man has lived under it for many centuries with the lamentable result of misery for the majority."

The undesirable consequences of this system of tenure, continued the pamphlet, were due to the small proprietor's lack of capital resources. His poverty forced him to rely upon usurers who lent money in return for a mortgage on the land or who bought the crop in advance on highly advantageous terms. The usurer soon took possession of the lot in lieu of payment of debts and, by repeating this procedure with many small proprietors, converted himself in time into a large landowner.

In order to prevent this monopolization of the land, continued the pamphlet, the Agrarian Law of October 26, 1915, prohibited the alienation of parcels in any form. But an important question remained. "How does a proprietor who has received a lot sow if he does not have the means to subsist until the harvest arrives?" The pamphlet offered two solutions: the creation and extension of agricultural credit and the stimulation of mutual help by the formation of cooperative societies among the small proprietors.

The Ministry of Agriculture and Colonization, the pamphlet promised, would found an agricultural credit bank shortly in order to make it unnecessary for the small agriculturalists to sell their crops on disadvantageous terms before harvest time and to enable them to improve their parcels and their crops.

The pamphlet recommended to the peasants the formation of two types of cooperative societies — consumers' cooperatives and producers' cooperatives. The members of the consumers' cooperatives would contribute money to a common fund, which in turn would be used to purchase articles of primary necessity; these articles would be distributed among the members in accordance with the monetary contribution each had made. In this way, the members would obtain articles of better quality and at lower cost.

The members of the producers' cooperatives would retain title to their respective parcels but they would work the land cooperatively. In addition to being more efficient than individual exploitation, this joining together of forces would enable the members to purchase, at wholesale prices, modern machinery such as thrashers and modern plows as well as breed animals and seed grain. It would be impossible for the individual proprietor to make such purchases. Also, by jointly marketing their products the members of the cooperative could obtain lower freightage costs and could afford to ship their grain to the markets which offered the highest prices. Thus, claimed the pamphlet, "this system does not have the inconveniences of the system of land keepers, nor the disadvantages of the isolated proprietor."

It is evident from this pamphlet that the *zapatistas* were partial to the small private property in the countryside, but it is also clear that they realized the shortcomings of that form of tenure. Hence, they suggested the formation of consumers' and producers' cooperatives in order to overcome the obstacles which small properties raised for the application to agricultural production of the achievements of modern science and technology and to overcome the problem of exploitation of the small proprietors by intermediaries.

The *zapatistas* attempted to implement their program of agrarian reform in the regions under their control and it appears that they distributed an extensive amount of land.[18] The peasants began to partition land among themselves as early as 1911;[19] in July, 1913, Zapata ordered his chieftains and officers to initiate the agrarian reform in the areas which they controlled, in the following terms: "The villages in general should take possession of their lands provided they have their corresponding property titles, in the manner stipulated in Article VI of the Plan of Ayala. The chiefs, as well as the officers, will lend their moral and material assistence to said villages in order that the depositions of the Plan of Ayala be fulfilled, in the case that villages solicit such help."[20] According to one of Zapata's principal associates, Antonio Díaz Soto y Gama, this order was carried out with the result that many villages recovered their lands.[21]

In a letter to President Woodrow Wilson dated August 23, 1914, Zapata declared the people were taking possession of the land in many areas of Mexico, as in Morelos, Guerrero, Michoacán, Puebla, Tamaulipas, Nuevo León, Chihuahua, Sonora, Durango, Zacatecas, and San Luís Potosí.[22]

Agrarian commissions were formed in the states of Morelos, Guerrero and Puebla toward the end of 1914 and early in 1915. In accordance with the provisions of the Agrarian Law of October 26, 1915, the commissions, composed largely of advanced students at the National School of Agriculture, carried out an intensive program of delineation and division of lands during 1915-1916 in states where *zapatista* influence predominated. In addition to dividing lands, the commissions fixed the boundaries of villages which already had taken possession of lands and, in the process, settled boundary disputes between villages.*[23]

*Villages which received lands or had their boundary disputes settled by these agrarian commissions included those of Santa María, Yautepec, Cuernavaca, Cocoyac, Huaxtepec, Itzmamatitlán, San Nicolás del Monte, Tlalnepantla, Tetecala, Miacatlán, Coatetelco, and Puente de Ixtla in Morelos; and of Taxco, El Naranjo, Platanillo, Tonalapa del Norte, Iguala, Tepecuacuilco and Tlaxmalac in Guerrero.

In addition to promoting the division of lands among individuals and communities, the revolutionaries of the South formed an agricultural credit bank (*Caja Rural de Préstamos*). The bank was financed initially, in part, from funds derived from the sale of urban properties expropriated from counterrevolutionaries. The bank made loans to villages for the purchase of tools, work animals and seed and for the maintenance of the agriculturalists from planting to harvest time. The bank also controlled several sugar mills in which it ground the peasants' cane at low cost.[24] In order to finance its operations the bank felt itself obliged to take possession of the sugar plantations which several *zapatista* chieftains were operating in order to acquire funds to maintain their troops. In this respect, Felipe Santibáñez, the principal author of the *zapatista* scheme of agricultural credit, has said "it should be said very loudly: the military chieftains did not cause any difficulties over surrendering the mentioned haciendas."

In his report on the labors of the agricultural credit bank in Morelos, Santibáñez declared that "The division of lands and the establishment of the Rural Credit Bank in the state of Morelos made it possible that the immense majority of the lands of said entity were cultivated by small landholders during the years 1915 and 1916, providing these smallholders with economic independence and resulting prosperity. It was notable that there was one small-scale agriculturalist who obtained on this plan a profit of 30,000 pesos in the currency of that epoch."[25]

Zapata placed considerable emphasis upon the sugar industry, encouraging the peasants to plant cane. He saw to it that the profits of the state-owned mill located near Cuautla went to the maintenance of his troops and to the relief of the poor. He left the greater part of the sugar mills in private hands, however, because the revolutionaries lacked the capital to reopen and operate all the mills in Morelos. In accordance with the provisions of the Plan of Ayala, however, the greater part of the lands of these sugar mills was expropriated and divided among the peasants. The mills, therefore, fulfilled in large part only their function as factories and were prevented from converting themselves into large landowners. Zapata expected that competition between millowners would maintain adequate prices for the cultivators; if not, the peasants would install small mills of their own to produce various forms of crude sugar.[26]

In interviews published in Havana newspapers in 1917 and 1918, General Jenaro Amezcua, whom Zapata sent to Havana in 1916 to propagandize the *zapatista* cause internationally, declared that Zapata began to divide the latifundia lands in small lots among the peasants shortly after he initiated the armed movement in the South in 1911. Amezcua claimed that the latifundia had disappeared and every citizen had a piece of land to cultivate in the regions which the *zapatistas* controlled. Land had also been distributed among peasant women, especially among the widows and orphans of revolutionaries. States affected by the land reform included Morelos, Guerrero, Puebla, Oaxaca, Vera Cruz, Tlaxcala and Hidalgo.[27]

Finally, in a "Call to the People" in August, 1918, Zapata declared:

"Furthermore, Carranza, instead of satisfying national aspirations by resolving the agrarian and worker problem by distributing land or dividing the large estates into fractions by means of amply liberal legislation; instead of doing this, I repeat, he has restored their numerous country places to the *hacendados* and large landowners which in another epoch were intervened by the Revolution . . . .

"On the other hand the Agrarian Revolution has made concrete promises and the humble classes have verified with experience that these offers are made effective. The Revolution distributes lands to the peasants and endeavors to improve the conditions of the city workers. No one fails to recognize this great truth. In the region occupied by the Revolution, haciendas and latifundia do not exist because General Headquarters has carried out their division in favor of the needy, apart from the return of their communal lands (*ejidos*) and rural properties to the villages and other neighboring communities."[28]

Lands expropriated by the *zapatistas* and other revolutionaries, of course, were liable to repossession after federal victories. The *carrancista* general, Pablo González, in his cruel campaign against the *zapatistas* during 1916, destroyed the sugar mills, pulled up the newly planted cane and, in general, destroyed the crops, work animals and habitations of the peasants. Although the Army of the South regained control of Morelos early in 1917, the Constitutionalists renewed their vicious attacks in 1918. The vicisitudes of warfare, therefore, always made it difficult for the men of the South to realize their plans for the permanent division of lands and the economic development of the countryside.[29]

Was it in fact necessary to carry out a thoroughgoing land reform in Mexico in order for that nation to continue its economic and human development? Indeed, it was. The destruction of the semi-feudal mode of production in agriculture was essential in order to develop a domestic market for industrial goods in the countryside, to promote the production of food and raw materials for industry, and to create a mobile labor supply. Mexico could not industrialize unless it achieved these objectives. Furthermore, in order to restrict the political influence of the owners of semi-feudal estates, it was necessary to limit their economic power through land reform.

The distribution of land sought by the *zapatistas*, therefore, would have stimulated Mexico's economic development considerably. The land distribution undertaken in the Cárdenas period (1934-1940) (which was anticipated by important reforms in the period from 1920-1934) had such an effect, and the salutary effects probably would have been much greater if the reform had been made two decades earlier.

The distribution of land, nevertheless, also has its negative aspects, especially if it is carried too far. That is to say, although it was a progressive measure to distribute land widely among small holders in the 18th and 19th centuries, in the second decade of the 20th century such a procedure was at least in part un-

economical, unless it was followed immediately by steps to reconcentrate the units of land under cultivation. Science and
technology by the early 20th century had made the cultivation
of certain commercial crops economical only if carried out on a
relatively large scale; wheat cultivation, for example, had reached
such a degree of development. In addition, small holders in a
capitalist society are at the mercy of commercial, financial
and industrial intermediaries, who exploit the small agriculturalists unmercifully and thereby prevent them from accumulat-
ing capital resources with which to improve the productivity
of their parcels.

As far as the cultivation of sugar in Morelos is concerned,
one can debate whether or not it was economical to divide the
sugar estates among small holders. Sugar production in Morelos
was industrialized only in the processing phase; the planting
and harvesting of the cane was done by primitive hand-labor
methods. Under these primitive technological conditions of
production, the peasant proprietor could produce as efficiently,
if not more so, as a large owner. Indeed, Mexico's sugar industry
has developed considerably since the revolution precisely upon
the basis of small units of production; that is to say, most of
Mexico's sugar-producing lands are organized into *ejidos*. The
two major shortcomings of this type of productive organization
are being felt now in Mexico: it makes the introduction of
costly technology unprofitable and it puts the small holder at
the mercy of those who own or control the sugar mills. Over the
years, the owners of the sugar mills in Mexico, whether private
capitalists or the federal government, have exploited the peasant
producers unmercifully. The regime of Adolfo López Mateos
(1958-1964) took the first steps to alleviate the conditions of
the peasant cane producers, incorporating them into Mexico's
social security program.

A number of crops in addition to sugar cane were raised in
Morelos, however. Many of these crops, such as corn and tobacco, could be cultivated efficiently on a small scale, especially
if adequate credit was available for the purchase of seed and tools,

and to maintain the agriculturalists before the harvest. As noted, the *zapatistas* created an agricultural credit bank to meet just these needs.

As we have seen, the *zapatistas* were well aware that small productive units restricted the application to agricultural production of the advances of modern science and technology and exposed the small owners to exploitation by intermediaries; they suggested the formation of consumers' and producers' cooperatives in order to overcome these negative aspects of small holdings in land. Also, it is worth emphasizing that the *zapatistas* did not look to the parceling of Mexico's agricultural lands into minuscule plots. Their Agrarian Law of October 26, 1915, permitted private individuals to possess rural properties which ranged in size from a maximum of 100 hectares in those areas most suitable to agricultural production to 1,500 hectares in those least suitable. Properties of this size would have permitted the flourishing of a capitalist agriculture in Mexico.

The agrarian reform undertaken by the regimes in power since 1920 has had largely beneficial effects upon Mexico's economic development. Nevertheless, the land reform, which in practice fell considerably short — to say the least — of fulfilling the *zapatista* program to protect the small producer from intermediaries, to make his labor more productive, and to provide him with adequate credit, has also had its negative consequences. Under the terms of modern technology, agricultural production has to be revolutionized quite rapidly in order to meet the requirements of a modern program of economic development. Modern technology permits the rapid revolutionizing of industrial production and, unless agriculture more or less keeps pace, great imbalances will arise in the economy which will threaten the entire program of development. That is precisely what has happened in Mexico. Mexico would had to have formed collectives and state farms in those regions of commercial crop production to have avoided or at least mitigated these problems. None of the major revolutionary factions called for such measures, although the *zapatistas* looked in that direction more than any other faction. That is to say, they recognized the negative aspects of small units of production in agriculture and, as a remedy, suggested the formation of consumers' and producers' cooperatives as well as the creation of an effective system of agricultural credit. Some 500 agricultural cooperatives were organized during the presidency of General Lázaro Cárdenas, but they were broken up in succeeding presidential regimes by bourgeois opponents of collectivization.

Given the fact that the collectivization of agriculture was an unlikely outcome of the Mexican Revolution of 1910, the distribution of at least a great part of the land among smallholders was the most feasible solution to Mexico's agrarian problem. Mexico's economic development was hampered because the *zapatista* proposals for land reform were not implemented throughout the nation. The problems of the countryside remain as the rock upon which Mexico's modern development program may flounder.

CHAPTER III

Liberalism And Anti-Imperialism

Political reform and agrarian reform can bring the peace and well-being which is desired.
— Emiliano   Zapata

Although land reform was their principal objective, Zapata and his men did not consider the distribution of land among the peasants as an end in itself. Land reform would free the peasant from the domination of the *hacendado* and would undermine his political influence to the degree that it destroyed his economic power. The economic liberation of the peasant and the destruction of the power of the landlords through land reform would provide the bases not only for improvements in the material conditions of the great mass of the Mexican people but also for their political, cultural and spiritual liberation. Thoroughgoing land reform, thought the *zapatistas,* would bring higher standards of living, greater equality of opportunity, the spread of popular education, political democracy and greater national independence. In addition to its antifeudal character, the revolution of the South was anti-imperialist and bourgeois-democratic. (These terms will be defined shortly.)

The basic theme that the destruction of Mexico's semi-feudal social structure through the distribution of land would enable Mexicans to achieve not only economic, but also political and spiritual liberation, runs through all the manifestations of *zapatista* thought. We shall present only a few examples.

Zapata saw the Plan of Ayala as an indispensable complement to Madero's Plan of San Luís. The latter plan, whose spirit was summed up in the motto "effective suffrage and no reelection," sought to make effective the reign of the liberal-bourgeois Constitution of 1857, which provided for a political democracy with individual guarantees in Mexico.[1] Article IV of the Plan of Ayala declared: "The Revolutionary Junta of the state of Morelos manifests to the nation under formal protest: That it makes the Plan of San Luís Potosí its own with the following additions which are expressed in benefit of the oppressed *pueblos*, and the Revolutionary Junta will make itself the defender of the principles which the Plan of San Luís defends until it conquers or dies."[2]

The principal objective of Zapata's Plan — in addition, of course, to its general purpose of denouncing Madero as a traitor to the revolution — was to extend, clarify and strengthen the weak agrarian provisions of Madero's Plan, which limited itself to calling for the restitution to small proprietors of lands which had been taken from them illegally. In short, the economic content of the Plan of Ayala was to complement the almost purely political content of the Plan of San Luís. Zapata made his intentions even clearer when he introduced the provisions for land reform of his Plan with the statement that "As an additional part of the Plan [of San Luís] which we invoke, we make known. . ."

The Act of Ratification of the Plan of Ayala of June 19, 1914, reiterated the assertion that Zapata's Plan was a complement to the Plan of San Luís. The Act began by stating: "The undersigned, chiefs and officers of the Liberator Army which fights for the fulfillment of the Plan of Ayala, *added to that of San Luís*. . ." (Italics added.) Further on, the Act declared that the revolution sought primarily to improve the economic conditions of the mass of oppressed Mexicans. A mere change in political rulers would not suffice to that end; the Mexican people could lift themselves from their misery only if they implemented the provisions of the Plan of Ayala, which was the "*complement and indispensable clarification of the Plan of San Luís Potosí.*" (Italics added.) The intention of Zapata's Plan, therefore, was to convert Madero's political revolution into a social revolution. The attainment of the economic objectives of the Plan of Ayala would permit the realization of the political ideals of the Plan of San Luís.

The Act concluded with the pledge that "The Revolution makes known that it will not consider its work finished until, with the present administration overthrown and the servants of *huertismo* and other personalities of the old regime eliminated from all participation in power, a government is established composed of men adhering to the Plan of Ayala who immediately carry into practice the agrarian reforms, as well as the other principles and promises included in the mentioned Plan of Ayala, added to that of San Luís."[3]

Zapata's manifesto of October 20, 1913, pledged that the *zapatistas* would continue their armed struggle until the revolution achieved profound changes in Mexico's institutional structure so as to provide for "economic liberty" and improved levels of living for the masses, for a just social and political order, and for a free, peaceful and civilized future for the Mexican nation.[4]

A manifesto which Zapata issued in August 1914 declared that the peasant launched into revolt to obtain land and bread and to regain his dignity. He sought "food and freedom, a happy home and a future of independence and aggrandizement." If the revolution was genuinely to triumph, it was necessary to undermine the sources of power of the reactionaries and to create new forces whose interests were linked with the destiny of the revolution. The former objective could be achieved by confiscating the property of the enemies of the revolution; the latter by distributing land among individuals and communities. Other reforms — freedom of the press and of suffrage, and Carranza's "timid reforms" which provided for municipal freedom and the abolition of estate-owned or "company" stores (*tiendas de raya*) — were illusory unless accompanied by these fundamental reforms in the economic structure of the nation. The great mass of the Mexican people could progress only by destroying the semi-feudal social order which oppressed them.

"The people of the countryside WANT TO LIVE THE LIFE OF CIVILIZATION, THEY TRY TO BREATH THE AIR OF ECONOMIC LIBERTY, which they have not known until now and which they can never attain if the traditional 'lord of the rope and knife' remains standing, disposing at his will of people and their labor, extorting them with the norm of their salaries, annihilating them with excessive labor, BRUTAL-IZING them with misery and bad treatment, diminishing and exhausting his race with the slow agony of servitude, with the forced withering of beings WHO ARE HUNGRY OF STOM-ACH AND MIND, WHICH ARE EMPTY."[5]

The *zapatistas* revealed their recognition of the intimate relationship between economic and political reform in a law providing for democratic political reform which the Convention government promulgated in Cuernavaca on January 8, 1916. The preamble to the law declared:

"It has been said that respecting the people, it is urgent that their civil rights be recognized and respected and that their political rights are a matter of scarce importance, and for this reason it is not urgent for the moment to take these rights into consideration. Lamentable error! Economic, political and social problems are intimately bound together, and one cannot be worthy the name of serious and formal statesman if he is not capable of comprehending that the solution of an economic or social problem never is correct if it is not in accordance with and related to the correlated and corresponding political problem. It is because of this that the National Executive Council, at the same time that it prepares the promulgation of laws in economic and social terms, does not ignore the study of those which it will have to promulgate in the political order to guarantee the future well being of the people."[6]

Thus, the *zapatistas* were intransigent in upholding the Plan of Ayala as their banner because they considered that the attainment of all revolutionary goals—economic development, more equitable distribution of wealth, higher standards of living, equality of opportunity and individual and social self-determination—depended upon the realization of the reforms in the property relationships of the nation which their Plan envisioned. Zapata made no fundamental changes or additions to his Plan not because he thought it could not be improved—the Agrarian

Law of October 26, 1915, broadened and made more precise the agrarian dispositions of the Plan of Ayala—but because he wished to base his revolutionary movement on firm principles and perhaps feared that he might disconcert his followers if he made changes in their banner. Thus, Zapata declared in a letter to Pascual Orozco, Jr. dated April 7, 1913, that he did not want to imprison himself behind "the unsurmountable barricade of a political plan" but it was necessary, he implied, to adhere closely to a plan accepted by all in order to avoid personalism and opportunism in revolutionary conduct.[7]

What was the specific content of the liberal-bourgeois and anti-imperialist reforms which the *zapatistas* sought? Before answering this question it would be well to clarify that the characteristic features of "liberal-bourgeois" or "bourgeois-democratic" thought are emphasis upon a wide distribution of property ownership, upon representative government with separation of powers, and upon individual guarantees; a liberal or bourgeois democracy is a democracy of small property owners. Imperialism, as used here, refers to the policy or practice of imposing one nation's or people's economic or political control upon another nation or people.

The men of the South gave evidence of the liberal-democratic and anti-imperialist tendencies of their thought as early as 1911. In March of that year, the Mexican government suppressed a revolutionary group composed of petty-bourgeois intellectuals, professionals, and urban workers which attempted to initiate an uprising against the Díaz regime. Members of the group, which was led by an engineer, Camilo Arriaga, included Francisco J. Mújica, later to become a Constitutionalist general, and José Vasconcelos.

The group's Political and Social Plan recognized Madero as the provisional president of Mexico and proclaimed the Constitution of 1857 and the principles of effective suffrage and no reelection as the supreme law of the land. It called for the restitution to the original owners of all lands usurped from them during the Díaz administration and ordered landowners to cede un-

cultivated lands to those who solicited them in return for annual
interest payments amounting to six per cent of the fiscal value
of the land. The Plan went on to provide, among other things, for
limitation of the work day to a maximum of nine hours and a
minimum of eight; formation of special commissions to regulate
wages "according to the yields of capital"; establishment of urban rent controls to prevent abuses of the poor by landlords and
pending the construction of "hygienic and comfortable habitations" which workers could purchase on easy terms; decentrali-
zation of public education. It also demanded regulation of the employment practices of foreign enterprises in Mexico: at least 50
per cent of the administrative and other employees of these foreign concerns had to be Mexicans and their salaries and bene-
fits had to be comparable to those of foreigners performing equal
work. Abolition of monopolies "of whatever character they may
be" was urged.[8] Although it did not mention them specifically,
this last proposal would have applied especially to foreign capitalist enterprises in Mexico. The Plan, in short, was anti-feudal,
bourgeois-democratic and anti-imperialist in character.

Rodolfo Magaña, who later became a *zapatista* general, took
a copy of the Plan to Zapata after the group was suppressed
in Mexico City. Zapata was attracted principally by the provisions for land reform, but evidently the entire Plan was to his
liking because he requested Magana to invite the remaining members of the revolutionary group to join his movement. There was
no response to the invitation at that time because the group had
been dispersed and some of its members were in prison. After
the victory of the Madero revolution, however, several members
were able to attend a dinner which Zapata gave in their honor in
Cuernavaca. Zapata exhorted these individuals to continue to
struggle for the realization of the principles of their Plan, especially those pertaining to land reform. Several members later
joined Zapata's movement, including Dolores Jiménez y Muro,
who had drafted the Plan, and Gildardo Magaña.[9]

The Program of Politico-Social Reforms of the Convention

government contains a detailed statement of the reforms which the *zapatistas* contemplated putting into effect.[10] Although *villistas* participated in formulating it in the Convention debates in 1914-1915, the Program may be considered to reflect *zapatista* thought since the men of the South completely dominated the Convention by the time it was issued in Cuernavaca in the spring of 1916 and furthermore, they fought to realize the Program.

The Program was divided into agrarian, labor, social, administrative, political and miscellaneous sections. Land reform, placed at the beginning of the document (and followed immediately by labor reform), envisioned the destruction of *latifundismo,* the parcelling of land in small, individual properties among all Mexicans who needed and requested land to support themselves and their families, and the granting of *ejidos* and natural sources of water to towns which in the past had been dispossessed of their lands or which did not have sufficient lands for their needs. In addition, this section called for the founding of agricultural banks; for investments in irrigation works, reforestation programs and means of communication; and for the establishment of regional agricultural experimental stations. Although the Program spoke of granting small properties to individuals, it is possible, in view of the provisions of the extensive Agrarian Law of October 26, 1915, discussed in the previous chapter, that the intention was to grant these lands in usufruct only and to prevent their sale or alienation in any form.

The rights and the well-being of the working class were considered in a section which called for regulation of wages and hours, accident and retirement pensions, safety and health measures in the workshops, factories and mines, legalizing of unions and the right to strike and boycott, abolition of *tiendas de raya,* prohibition of the practice of paying wages in token, legislation to ensure the prompt payment of wages, and, in general, the improvement of the workers' conditions "by means of legislation which makes the exploitation of the proletariat less cruel."

The remaining articles of the Program dealt with social, administrative and political reforms. The Convention announced its intention in these articles, among other things, to safeguard the rights of illegitimate children and to emancipate women by means of an equitable divorce law. In the area of education to establish elementary schools which emphasize physical, manual and practical training; to organize normal schools in every state; to raise teacher's salaries; to emancipate the National University, and to give preference to manual arts and industrial science in higher education.

With respect to law and the legal position of corporations, to reform the common law and to make the administration of justice "expeditious and effective"; to destroy existing monopolies and prevent the creation of new ones; to reform corporation law to protect minority stockholders and to prevent abuses by the corporation directorates; to require foreign enterprises operating in Mexico to submit themselves to the jurisdiction of Mexican courts under all circumstances, to establish directorates in Mexico with the authority and obligation to pay dividends, to keep their shareholders well informed, and to make their accounts and other documents available to the public.

The Program also sought to reform mineral and petroleum laws in such manner as to promote the development of the mining and petroleum industries, to prevent the monopolizing of vast zones, to give the federal government participation in the gross production of these industries, and to require enterprises to work their concessions actively and efficiently and to protect the life and health of the workers on penalty of forfeiture of their concessions.

In the field of taxation, the Program undertook to exempt artisans, small merchants and private rural properties of small value from all taxes; to revise taxes, abolish personal or captation taxes, establish a progressive inheritance tax, free articles of primary necessity from indirect taxes, abolish the special tax privileges of the large capitalists, and reduce protective tariffs without hurting national industrial interests.

In the political domain, the Program sought to realize municipal independence; to adopt a parliamentary form of government; to abolish the vice-presidency, the national senate and the *jefaturas políticas* (regional or district units of government); to reorganize the judicial power in order to guarantee its independence and to ensure that its functionaries were able and responsible; to institute electoral reforms which would prevent electoral frauds and ensure direct voting in local and federal elections; and to punish the enemies of the revolution by confiscating their properties in accordance with legal procedures.

A final section of "transitory articles" gave the Sovereign Revolutionary Convention authority to ratify the nomination of the state governors. The Convention could deny ratification if the nomination was not made in accordance with the provisions which the Plan of Ayala contained on this matter (which shall be examined later in this chapter) or "if the candidate lacked revolutionary antecedents." The Convention could remove governors from office if they violated the precepts of the Plan of Ayala or of the Convention Program of reforms, or if they committed crimes or tolerated abuses by their subordinates, or if they accepted reactionary elements into their government. Only chieftains who began to participate in the revolution before the fall of Huerta could participate in the elections to name state governors.

The Program is anti-feudal, bourgeois-democratic and anti-imperialist in spirit. The Program manifests its anti-feudalism directly in the provisions for the division of large landed estates among smallholders and, indirectly, in a number of provisions which provide for the creation of a radical petty-bourgeois democracy in Mexico.

The radical petty-bourgeois nature of the intended reforms is revealed specifically in the following features of the Program: (1) It encouraged the creation of small, individual properties (although perhaps these properties were to be inalienable and held in usufruct only). (2) It intended to leave industry capitalistically organized and to permit foreign capitalist enterprises to operate in Mexico, although strictly subject to Mexican law. The big capitalists were to have some of their activities and prequisites restricted (*e.g.*, by prohibiting the formation of monopolies, by abolishing the tax privileges of the large capitalists, by establishing a progressive inheritance tax), while the owners of small properties were to have their rights and opportunities extended and protected (*e.g.*, by tax exemptions and protection of minority stockholders). (3) A parliamentary republic with separation of powers was to be established and, in general, the political life of the nation was to be democratized. The provisions which gave the Convention government authority to ratify nominations of the state governors and to depose these officials under certain circumstances were not in contradiction with the democratic spirit of the other proposed reforms. Considering the disorganized state of Mexican society after years of revolutionary struggle, such measures were undoubtedly necessary in order to thwart the counterrevolutionary maneuverings of reactionaries and to ensure that the governments which emerged in the states would be progressive and revolutionary.

The petty-bourgeois liberalism of the Program, however, differed in several respects from 19th century liberalism. The Program envisioned greater intervention by the state in the affairs of the nation than did traditional liberal doctrine and it called for social as well as individual guarantees for the Mexican people. The liberalism of the Program, therefore, is more consonant with the liberal ideology of 20th century state capitalism, which some have called "social liberalism," than with the liberal thought associated with 19th century *laissez faire* capitalism. "Social liberalism" is traditional liberalism with greater social consciousness; it advocates that the state in monopoly capitalist society play an active role in promoting economic development, in preventing critical disequilibriums from arising in the economy, and in looking after the well-being of all social classes. "Welfare capitalism," which some mistakenly label as "socialism," is the typical product of the new liberalism. The Convention Program contained features of both conceptions of liberalism. Its anti-monopoly provisions seemed to harken to 19th century liberal concepts, while its labor and social welfare provisions foreshadowed the new liberalism of state capitalism.

The *zapatista* Program predicated less intervention by the state in the economy than did the *carrancistas* subsequently in the Constitution of 1917. Consequently, traditional liberal thought concerning the role of the state in society appears to have influenced the *zapatista* document more than the Constitution. The Constitution of 1917, it may be recalled, asserted that the Mexican nation was the original owner of the national lands, waters and subsoil deposits. The national ownership of the subsoil and waters was inalienable, although the nation could grant concessions for their exploitation to private individuals. The nation at all times had the authority to impose upon private property the conditions and forms which social interest demanded and private property could be expropriated by reason of public utility. The concern expressed in the *zapatista* Program to control the exploitation of the subsoil and to limit the abuses of private property (*e.g.*, by placing restrictions on the operations of foreign enterprises in Mexico and by dividing large landed properties) is in accord with the spirit of these Constitutional precepts.

In addition to its anti-feudal and bourgeois-democratic character, the Program was anti-imperialist. The land reform would affect foreigners as well as nationals. The extensive labor reforms were applicable, realistically, only to large enterprises and most of these were owned by foreigners, *e.g.*, the textile mills and the smelters. Similarly, the anti-monopoly provisions would apply most immediately and directly to the large foreign corporations in Mexico. The provision which called for reforms in that nation's mineral and petroleum laws seems to reveal a desire on the part of the drafters of the Program to repossess Mexico's natural resources which were alineated to foreigners or, at least, to place restrictions and limitations upon foreign exploitation of these resources. Finally, foreign capitalist enterprises would be permitted to continue to operate in Mexico, but only on condition that they subjected themselves strictly to the norms of Mexican law. The fact that the Convention couched the anti-imperialist provisions of its Program in moderate tones or introduced them in an indirect, dissimulated form indicates, it seems to me, caution on the part of the Convention in face of the considerable power of American imperialism.

The Manifesto which accompanied the Program,[11] however, made quite clear the anti-imperialist — as well as the anti-feudal — sentiment of its drafters. It accused Carranza of complicity in the invasion of northern Mexico by U.S. troops under the command of General Pershing which had occurred in March 1916, shortly before the Manifesto and Program were issued, and went on to claim: "The ephemeral victories of our enemies are due to their immodest alliance with Mister Wilson, to the arms and munitions which the latter sends them, to the protection which he concedes to their forces so that they may enter and leave American territory."

The manifesto went on to claim that the Conventionists would attain victory in the end because the people were with them. It concluded:

"We divide the haciendas among the peasants; the *carrancistas* return them to the *hacendados* and join with them to combat those who ask for bread and lands.

"*Carrancismo* is treason twice over: treason because it has sold out the homeland; treason because it has sold out to the *hacendados*.

"Carranza, Wilson and the great landlords, then, are the enemies which the Mexican people have to overcome.

"The Revolutionary Convention invites the Mexican people to this great struggle."

There are numerous further examples of the bourgeois-democratic and anti-imperialist content of *zapatista* thought. In regards to the liberal-bourgeois orientation of the *zapatistas,* we have already noted that Zapata conceived the Plan of Ayala as an addition to Madero's Plan of San Luís, whose principal objective was to establish a political democracy in Mexico.

In addition, Zapata's Plan provided democratic means for reestablishing the nation's political order once the revolution had triumphed. A convention of the nation's principal revolutionary leaders was to name the provisional president of the republic, who in turn was to convoke general elections. The state governments were to be reestablished by a similar procedure. The principal revolutionary chieftains of each state were to nominate a provisional governor, who in turn was to hold elections. As noted previously, the provisions in the Convention Program which gave the Convention government authority to depose state governors in certain circumstances were intended to guarantee the revolutionary character of the state governments. Such measures were necessary to thwart the counterrevolution.

In their speeches before the Aguascalientes Convention, Antonio Díaz Soto y Gama and Paulino Martínez spoke of realizing political democracy, of guaranteeing civil liberties and of putting an end to the exploitation of the Mexican people by minorities. Martínez condemned clericalism, militarism and bossism (*caciquism*) which, he claimed, exploited the peasants in the countryside and the workers in the cities.[12]

The preamble to the law on political reform mentioned previously which the Convention government promulgated in Cuernavaca on January 8, 1916, reiterated what it declared to be the universally accepted principle that sovereignty resides essentially and originally with the people. It went on to point out that representative political bodies frequently abuse the popular sovereignty which gave birth to them and that, therefore, the Convention government thought it necessary to provide legislation which would strengthen the principle of popular sovereignty and assure that the people themselves determine the character of the institutions and laws upon which their prosperity and happiness depend. The accompanying law provided that "the fundamental laws of the Republic must be subjected to the ratification of the people expressed by means of the plebiscite." Once ratified by the people, the nation's laws must

be implemented punctually and without evasions by the authorities. Finally, the law recognized the people's right to rebellion
(*derecho de rebelión*) in order to overthrow political authorities
who abused the popular sovereignty.[13]

Sergio Valverde, a communications officer in the Liberator
Army of the South, has quoted Zapata as saying in private conversation in the spring of 1916 that the Plan of Ayala had supported that of San Luís primarily because the latter upheld the
principles of effective suffrage and no reelection. Adherence to
these principles in practice, claimed Zapata, would prevent the
formation of oligarchies which use the state power to tyrannize
and exploit the people. Hence, according to Zapata, the observa-
tion of these political principles would ensure the social con-
quests of the revolution.[14]

Zapata issued an Exposition to the Mexican People and to the
Diplomatic Corps on October 1, 1916.[15] It denounced Carranza
as a farcical despot who had deceived the Mexican people with
false revolutionary promises. Once Carranza had attained power,
he violated all his promises. He returned lands to hacendados;
broke workers' strikes, closed the *Casa del Obrero Mundial*
(described below), and jailed the more militant workers; restricted freedom of expression; violated systematically the freedom of the ballot; restricted the freedom of commerce; created
chaos and hardship with his financial measures; and institutional-
ized corruption, despoliation of the weak, assasination of opponents, personalism and praetorianism as methods as government.

Zapata expressed his belief in freedom of religious consciousness and at the same time revealed that he recognized the de-
mogogic and counterrevolutionary spirit of much of the anti-
religious propaganda and activities of the Constitutionalists.
Carranza's movement, according to Zapata, had unleashed
an anti-religious campaign—which included the invasion of
churches, the burning of confessionals and the destruction of
Saints' images—in order to conceal the lack of revolutionary
content in its economic and social programs. Zapata claimed,
with profound prevision, that "these attacks upon the religious

cult and the popular conscience are counterproductive and prejudicial because they persuade no one, they convince no one. They only exacerbate passions, create martyrs, awaken more vividly the superstitions which they wish to dominate and give strength to the enemy whom they pretend to fight." Zapata went on to indicate that the revolution was basically anti-feudal in content, not anti-religious or anti-clerical. The revolution was essentially economic; it sought to destroy the large estates and free the rural workers from feudal slavery and "to protect the city workers against the avidity of the capitalists." As former *zapatista* Octavio Paz has explained, Zapata's views on religion were "entirely liberal" but he considered the best way to end religious fanaticism among the people was by persuasion and education, not by force.[16]

Zapata gave further expression in this document to the bourgeois-democratic spirit of his movement. He protested violations by the *carrancistas* of the freedoms of press, expression, suffrage, and commerce, and he defended the worker's right to organize and to strike. Zapata claimed that the revolution had the support of the "indigenous race" (the ethnic groups of pre-Cortesian origins), the peasants, the workers and "of all people of work and enterprise, whether they be merchants, industrialists or simple working people" because these social groups had seen that the revolution fulfills its promises. The revolution, continued the Manifesto, distributes lands, protects commerce, undertakes the redemption of the Indians, and offers a broad program of social rights to the workers, which includes the right to form unions, to strike, and to use a great variety of means to defend themselves against their employers.

Zapata issued another manifesto on January 20, 1917,[17] which stated the objectives of the revolution in the broad terms of his manifesto of the previous October. The revolution, stated Zapata, sought to distribute the land and free the peasant. It offered generous and ample reforms and guarantees to the peasant and the worker; regeneration and freedom of commerce; facilities and guarantees to industry and banking; and, to the

Mexican people in general, protection against the formation of monopolies and "solid and meditated reforms on the basis of our present culture." Carranza, on the other hand, offered destruction, despoliation, autocracy, and the continued domination of Mexico by the hacendado and the *cacique,* "the true enemies of civilization and of our race."

Zapata issued a lengthy Manifesto to the People on April 20, 1917,[18] which, while sustaining fulfillment of the economic principles of the Plan of Ayala as the key to the success of the social revolution, also reflected the broader objectives of the revolution of the South. This manifesto, as previous ones, declared that the revolution sought to unite Mexicans under a generous policy; it gave guarantees to workers, peasants, merchants and industrialists; it criticized the arbitrary, personalist and unpopular nature of the Carranza regime; and it declared that the principal aim of the revolution was to destroy the latifundia system and its consequent evils and to establish a popular political regime which would guarantee order, liberty and justice.

Zapata issued a Protest before the Mexican People on May 1, 1917,[19] in which he denounced Carranza's assumption of the presidency of the republic on that date as a farce and a fraud. Even Huerta, declared Zapata, attempted to give his rigged elections the appearance of genuine electoral struggle. Carranza dropped even the pretense of democracy and forced his opponents to renounce their candidacy and support his own. "Under these conditions, the election was an insult to the dignity of all and a betrayal of principles proclaimed a hundred times over." In imposing himself upon the Mexican people in an electoral farce, Carranza violated the promise he made in the Plan of Guadalupe and in his Veracruz decrees to renounce his title as "First Chief" and deliver his authority into the hands of a chief executive elected by the people. Carranza perpetrated the farce of dispossessing himself of his title of "First Chief" only to assume that of "President of the Republic," thereby delivering the executive power of the nation to himself. Zapata passed the following judgement on Carranza:

"In Carranza's opinion the triumph of the revolution can be reduced to his personal triumph and, although there are no lands divided, nor guarantees conceded to the people, nor effective improvement of the peasant and the worker, the revolution has concluded by the single fact that he has become the supreme political authority, blindly obeyed by a group of servile followers who form a faction which the entire Republic detests."

Zapata offered another biting estimation of Carranza's character in the following paragraph from a manifesto dated February 27, 1918:[20]

"Popular instinct had not been deceived, peasant intuition was right. Carranza, man of antechambers, legitimate creature of the past, imbued in the teachings of the *porfirista* court, accustomed to the ideas and practices of servilism and autocracy, understanding politics as the art of deceiving and considering as the best of all rulers he who with most assuredness knows how to impose his all-embracing will; Carranza the antiquated, Carranza the ancient, was not in condition to understand the new times and the new aspirations."

The *zapatista* organ, *El Sur,* which was published at the general headquarters of the Liberator Army of the South at Tlaltizapán, Morelos, frequently referred to labor problems. For example, an article which appeared in *El Sur* on April 20, 1918,[21] roundly denounced Carranza for deceiving the workers with his labor legislation. On the one hand, Carranza conceded all sorts of rights to the workers while on the other he declared that only those strikes which sought to harmonize the rights of labor and capital were licit. In regards to this latter possibility, the article declared: "Harmonize the rights of the exploiter and the exploited! Conciliate abuse with right, iniquity with justice, innocence with guilt, the iniquity of the slave traders of the 20th century with the sacrosanct rights of the proletarians, the authors of civilization and the creators of human wealth!"

By giving the government the option to declare strikes illegal, continued the article, Carranza had effectively destroyed the right to strike and thereby placed the worker at the mercy of the capitalist. Furthermore, the stipulation in Article 123 of the Constitution of 1917 that employers may dismiss workers for just cause permitted employers to fire any worker they chose because a "just cause" could always be found. In addition, continued the article, employers had formed blacklists of workers they considered troublesome and denied these workers employment everywhere. The article concluded: "How much—and how many—magnates must be blessing Carranza for his 'beneficent' laws which offer such precious guarantees to the rich against the poor and to the powerful against the humble!"

Zapata issued what turned out to be his last manifesto on March 17, 1919, in the form of an open letter to Carranza.[22] As was the case with his previous manifestos, the scope was broad and he went in detail into the problems of the proletariat. He criticized the Carranza regime for undermining and destroying the effectiveness of labor unions—"the only defense, the principal bastion of the proletariat in the struggles which it has to undertake for its improvement"—and for subjugating the unions to governmental manipulation and control.

As these manifestos and programs indicate, therefore, the *zapatistas* wished to establish a political democracy in Mexico which would guarantee rights to the various social classes. These guarantees, however, such as those offered to the working class, were intended to protect the interests of individuals and groups within capitalist society; they did not envision an end to capitalist property relationships. Indeed, the *zapatista* program, which sought to destroy semi-feudal social relationships in the countryside and to stimulate small private enterprises of every sort, would have removed obstacles to the development of capitalism in Mexico.

Zapata, however, apparently recognized that capitalism was only a temporary stage of social organization in the course of human development. Thus, in defending "freedom of commerce," *e.g.*, the untrammeled exchange of commodities on the domestic market, in the Exposition to the Mexican People and to the Diplomatic Corps which he issued on October 1, 1916, Zapata declared: "Carranza forgot that while the bourgeois stage sub-sists, and we find ourselves in it, whether we want to be or not, one of the fundamental laws of this type of social organization, today the dominant one by the fatality of evolution, is and must be the principle of freedom of commerce."[23]

We have noted the anti-imperialist features of the Convention program of social and political reforms of 1916 and of the revolutionary plan which a group of intellectuals and workers issued in Mexico City in 1911 and with which Zapata sympathized. The *zapatistas* gave many other indications of the anti-imperialist orientation of their movement.

The preamble to the famous *zapatista* manifesto of October 20, 1913, complained that the agricultural and mineral wealth of the nation was controlled by a few thousand capitalists "and of these a great part are not Mexicans." With the connivance of the courts and the assistance of the government and the army, these capitalists robbed the workers and the peons of their labor and their lands. No specific mention was made of industrial wealth, although the manifesto did denounce the bourgeoisie which "robs the worker and the peon of the product of his labor." Although the manifesto did not mention the United States when it criticized foreign capitalists, it was well known by all that American capitalists were the principal foreign investors in Mexico.[24]

In the only statement with anti-imperialist content in his Exposition to the Mexican People and to the Diplomatic Corps dated October 1, 1916, Zapata announced to the Diplomatic Corps that the revolution did not recognize and formally declared null and void "the treaties, agreements and conventions which *carrancismo* undertakes with foreign powers or with private individuals of other countries, whether it is a question of indemnities, concessions, loans or any other class of af-fairs."[25] Although this declaration was obviously made with the intent to undermine the confidence of foreign governments and foreign investors in the Carranza regime and although it was standard procedure for opponents of a regime to make similar declarations, it also appears to reflect concern on the part of the *zapatistas* over the concessions the *carrancistas* might make to foreign imperialism.

In his Manifesto to the People dated April 20, 1917, Zapata claimed that the Carranza regime had contracted "onerous and unworthy compromises with the potentates of the Republic or of foreign countries" in order to acquire money, arms and munitions to continue its war upon the popular forces of the revolution. The revolution of the South, in contrast, "never has gone to humiliate itself before a foreign government in order to solicit armaments, munitions or pecuniary resources like a beggar and, nevertheless, having to fight against an enemy endowed with powerful elements due to the favor of foreigners, it has been able to take, inch by inch, a vast zone of the Republic's territory from the enemy."[26]

Zapata again manifested his anti-imperialism, as well as his anti-feudalism, in the Protest before the Mexican People which he issued on May 1, 1917. He charged that Carranza had issued a manifesto in Vera Cruz which declared that the confiscations of the properties of enemies of the revolution were without foundation "with the sole purpose of gaining recognition from the North American government" and that Carranza had compromised himself indirectly to maintain the latifundia system when he declared that the large landowners would not have all their properties expropriated, "but only that minimum part which is considered convenient."[27] It is well to recall at this point that foreigners held extensive amounts of land in Mexico, including cattle ranches, coffee and rubber estates, sugar and tobacco plantations, and timber lands.

The following quotation from the Manifesto to the People which Zapata issued on April 20, 1917, summarizes the bourgeois-democratic and anti-imperialist, as well as the anti-feudal, character of the revolution of the South.

"To unite Mexicans by means of a generous and broad political policy which will give guarantees to the peasant and to the worker as well as to the merchant, the industrialist and the businessman;

to grant facilities to all who wish to improve their future and open wider horizons for their intelligence and their activities; to provide work to those who today lack it; to promote the establishment of new industries, of great centers of production, of powerful manufactures which will emancipate the country from the economic domination of the foreigner; to call everyone to the free exploitation of the land and of our natural riches; to alleviate misery in the home and to procure the moral and intellectual improvement of the workers, creating higher aspirations in them; such are the intentions which animate us in this new stage which has to lead us, surely, to the realization of the noble ideals maintained without dismay for seven years, in spite of all obstacles and at the cost of the greatest sacrifices."[28]

Considerable evidence exists to indicate that the *zapatistas* attempted to realize in practice some of the broader objectives mentioned in their programs and manifestos. In addition to dividing lands and promoting economic development in the areas under their control, the revolutionaries of the South concerned themselves with such problems as public education, health, and municipal freedom. There is also some indication that during the revolution Zapata attempted to put labor reforms into practice, thus to improve the conditions of urban workers in the regions under his control.[29] With regard to their anti-imperialism, it is worth noting that the *zapatistas* played no favorites in the distribution of lands, expropriating foreigners and nationals alike.

Zapata's Organic Municipal Law of April, 1917, provided autonomy for municipal administrations and prohibited the re-election of municipal authorities. It authorized the municipalities to grant contracts for the provision of public services and obliged fathers to send their children to school.[30] Municipal elections were held with absolute freedom in the regions controlled by the *zapatistas,* whereas "municipal freedom" was only a farce in the rest of the republic.[31]

Zapata had great interest in education and sought to establish primary schools in the municipalities located within the areas controlled by his forces, although the constant warfare and the lack of financial resources made it difficult to achieve this objective. Various *zapatista* circulars ordered municipalities to establish schools. In one of these circulars Zapata claimed:

"At the same time that our labarum of redemption is inscribed 'lands' in order to give the daily bread to the needy classes, in the same fashion 'civilization' is inscribed in order to give intellectual bread, also daily, to these same classes; from the first they will obtain nutrition and the development of their organism in order to be strong and from the second food and modulation of their spirit in order to be free and happy; ignorance and obscurantism in all ages have produced nothing but herds of slaves for tyrannies."[32]

In another circular dated August 22, 1917, Zapata declared: "Now, you know perfectly well that one of the ideals for which we are fighting is that of fomenting Public Education and if under the pretext that the times through which we are passing are abnormal we were to neglect such an important branch, we would contravene our own ideals, which should not happen for any reason."[33]

A circular dated April 17, 1917, noted that many villages had already established primary schools and that night schools for adults had been established in Fochimilco, Puebla, and in Jantetelco and Zacualpan, Morelos; a manual arts school was soon to open in Tochimizolco.[34]

In conclusion, the *zapatistas* sought to destroy Mexico's semi-feudal economic structure by distributing the hacienda's lands widely among the people. The wide distribution of land would provide the basis for more equitable distribution of income and for greater equality of opportunity among the Mexican people. It would also permit a more rational and intensive exploitation of the land, thereby promoting economic development and raising levels of living. Greater prosperity would permit the extension and improvement of educational facilities for the people. The wide distribution of property would undermine the political influence of the large landowners and pave the way for the creation of a democratic political regime which, in turn, would guarantee the rights of the peasants and other small owners, as well as of the proletariat. Similarly, the state would take measures to limit the influence of foreign imperialism in the nation's domestic affairs. Economic development, democratic control of the nation's economic and political life, and freedom from exploitation of man by man would make the Mexican people the masters of their fate. In the measure that they understood and therefore controlled their natural and social environment, the Mexican people would free themselves to develop their distinctively human potentialities to the full.

The basis of this structure of freedom which the *zapatistas* wished to create was the wide distribution of property among the people. Confronted, however, with the conditions of 20th century technology which had made impractical a thoroughgoing distribution of property, especially of industrial property, the *zapatistas* had to modify the terms of the traditional liberal, or Rousseauian-Jeffersonian, road to freedom in order to come to grips with modern technology and its complement, monopoly capitalism and imperialism. They did so by proposing a series of measures which would defend and promote the interests of small property owners and the proletariat within the framework of capitalist property relationships. The state was to guarantee certain rights to these classes and was also to protect the nation from foreign imperialism. These measures and guarantees included, among other things, the safeguarding of the small rural holder from expropriation by granting him only the usufruct to the land and by making his holding inalienable; the creation of consumers' and producers' cooperatives in the countryside in order to protect the small holder and make his labor more productive; the granting of tax exemptions to small owners and the abolition of tax privileges for the large owners; the reforming of corporate law to protect minority stockholders; the abolition of monopolies; the guaranteeing of a number of rights to the workers, including the right to organize, strike and boycott; the regulation by the state of the exploitation of the nation's natural resources; the strict subjection of foreign enterprises in Mexico to the jurisdiction of the national courts; and the creation of a parliamentary democracy and the subjection of the nation's laws to popular referendum in order to ensure popular control of the machinery of the state. In short, the liberalism of the *zapatistas* assumed aspects of contemporary social liberal thought.

CHAPTER IV

Misconceptions Concerning *Zapatista* Ideology

The enemies of the country and of freedom of the people have always denounced as bandits those who sacrifice themselves for the noble causes of the people. — Emiliano Zapata

The interpretation of *zapatista* ideology presented in this work contrasts with the views of some who have characterized Zapata's movement as displaying strong socialist, anarchist or "Indianist" features. The *zapatistas* undoubtedly were influenced by these concepts but, in this respect, one should be careful not to make a mountain out of a molehill. Indeed, when one examines the revolution of the South in all its manifestations, including its intellectual expressions, these interpretations appear tendentious.

The "Indianist" concept can be disposed of most easily. Howard Cline summed up the Indianist thesis when he wrote that "Zapata expected to exterminate all Europeanized Mexicans in southern Mexico and make of the land a milpa-studded collection of *ranchos* in the Indian mode."[1] The whole import of the material presented so far belies any such simple intention on the part of the *zapatistas* to return to a mestizo-less, creole-less, Indian-dominated social order. Their broadly conceived plans and programs for social reform, which were examined previously, substantiate this remark. Also, as Baltasar Dromundo indicates to belie the Indianist thesis, Zapata himself and the majority of the other leaders were mestizos.[2] Zapata wore the costume of the *charro* (cowboy or small rural proprietor), not the white *calzones* (breeches) typical of the Indian peon. He was a *ranchero*; the peasant village in which he was reared was not an Indian community *per se* similar, say, to those found in Oaxaca and Chiapas, in which all or mostly all of the residents speak an indigenous dialect as their native tongue and consider themselves members of their ethnic group firstly as Mexicans only secondarily, if at all. His favorite diversion, at which he excelled, was the *charreada* or rodeo, the typical sport of the mestizo *ranchero*. He had received at least a rudimentary education and had served in the federal army, where he had promptly achieved the rank of sergeant due to his outstanding ability to handle horses and to lead men. Former *zapatista* Octavio Paz, in describing Zapata's appearance, his fine *charro* costume, his elaborate saddles and his excellent horses, his pistol on his belt and his rifle in his hand, declared that Zapata "presented himself before the enthused crowds which followed him as the genuine representative of the true national type."[3]

According to the more subtle companion of the "Indianist" thesis, the *zapatistas* were concerned only with their region or *patria chica*. Their limited peasant mentality prevented them from grasping the larger military-strategic or political exigencies of the revolution. Because of their restricted outlook, continues this thesis, the *zapatistas* let pass many opportunities to engage and perhaps defeat the *carrancistas* in combat outside of their region.[4]

It is unquestionable that the revolutionaries of the South fought primarily for the redistribution of land and that the peasant's principal concern was with affairs in his own locality. Many of the military chieftains of the Army of the South — although not all — were rude and ignorant. In this respect, however, Zapata's forces did not differ from the other revolutionary armies which were composed largely of peasants and whose chieftains were often ignorant and cruel. These facts, nevertheless, do not necessarily imply that the *zapatistas* were incapable of comprehending that their local interests were linked inevitably with the destinies of the Mexican nation.

The ample scope, realism and profound revolutionary consciousness of the *zapatista* manifestos and proclamations and of their program of political and social reforms issued in 1916 belies the alleged circumscribed political outlook of the warriors of the South. The Plan of Ayala, issued as early as November 1911 and formulated almost wholly by Zapata himself, called for solutions to Mexico's economic and political problems on a national level. Indeed, Zapata demonstrated greater interest in implementing a program of thoroughgoing economic, social and political reforms throughout Mexico than did Villa or, especially, Carranza. Also, as we shall see in more detail in the next chapter, Zapata was concerned with the international prestige of his movement and sent agents abroad to propagandize the revolutionary cause and counteract what he considered to be the distortions and calumnies of *carrancista* propaganda.

We may speculate that if Zapata had been concerned only with the affairs of Morelos he might well have been able to reach an accord with Carranza in 1914 to permit a thoroughgoing land reform in the state of Morelos. Carranza would have attained the pacification of one of his major opponents at the cost of permitting agrarian reform along *zapatista* lines in one of the smallest states of the republic. In his negotiations with Madero in the summer of 1911, Zapata evidently was willing to disband his forces in return for a political and agrarian settlement in Morelos. His experiences at that time must have made him aware of the futility of seeking a purely local settlement for he contemptuously rejected Huerta's offer for such a settlement in 1913 and he never gave the slightest indication in later years that he might be ready to reconsider his decision. On the contrary, from the Plan of Ayala in 1911 to his last manifesto in 1919, as we have seen, Zapata invariably couched his demands for reform in national terms. He and his men insisted intransigently throughout the revolution that the other armed movements accept the principles of this plan as the price for reestablishing peace in Mexico.

Thus, although it is true, as Sotelo Inclán and Chevalier, among others, have indicated, that Zapata began his career as a local leader who defended the interests of his native village and that he thereby merely followed in the footsteps of peasant leaders who throughout the centuries had defended their village's interests, his measure as an historical personage rests precisely upon the fact that he grew in stature. Furthermore, in contrast to earlier peasant uprisings, Zapata's rebellion from its inception was leagued with a national revolutionary movement. Zapata passed from a local leader who defended his village's rights, to a regional leader who fought for the economic and political rights of the residents of his native state, to a national revolutionary leader who struggled to implement a program of thoroughgoing reforms throughout Mexico and who, as shall be apparent in the following chapter, employed a strategy conceived in national and even international terms in his attempt to achieve victory.

After overthrowing Carranza in 1920, Obregón made a settlement with the remaining *zapatistas* which was similar in terms to that which Zapata had sought from Madero in the summer of 1911. Land reform was pushed in Morelos, the *zapatista* general Genovevo de la O was named military commander of the state, and a medical doctor who had served as Zapata's physician was named governor. This purely local settlement represented a retreat from the principles of the Plan of Ayala. Nevertheless, this retreat was the only realistic alternative open to the remaining warriors of the South, considering that Zapata was dead, that Morelos and contiguous regions were devasted after ten years of struggle, and that the Liberator Army of the South possessed only a fraction of its former strength. It would be pure fantasy to suggest that the remaining *zapatistas* should have acted otherwise.

The public statements of the *zapatistas* were influenced by the concepts of the petty-bourgeois intellectuals associated with the movement. (The same was true of the public pronouncements of the other revolutionary factions.) However, as one of Zapata's closest intellectual collaborators, Díaz Soto y Gama, put it: "Of course, it was those of us who collaborated with him [Zapata] who gave more or less grammatical or literary form to said documents [Zapata's manifestos and proclamations]; but it was he who always gave the ideas which had to be developed."[5] Zapata, in short, dominated his movement and personally made all vital decisions in regards to ideological as well as to military and other practical matters.[6]

Octavio Paz, one of the more able of the intellectuals associated with the Army of the South has made interesting observations on Zapata's intellectual capacities. According to Paz, Zapata had "perfect understanding of the motives for which he sustained such a brave struggle" and discussed revolutionary problems and programs with ease and with profound understanding. Zapata had acquired a lively interest in books as a boy and was a ready learner; when he realized the significance of the role which he had to play in the revolution, he set about to further his instruction, dedicating two or three hours to reading every evening when he was at general headquarters in Tlaltizapán, Morelos. His favorite reading was history. Paz has also referred to the fact that the only one who might have been considered an intellectual among Zapata's associates during the first few years of his struggle was the former schoolteacher, Otilio Montaño, and he was "quite stupid." Nevertheless, it was during these years that Zapata issued the Plan of Ayala and responded in vibrant, revolutionary tone to Huerta's attempts to come to an understanding with him.[7]

The average *zapatista* may not have been able to articulate his goals as well as the intellectuals, nor to plan the precise political, administrative, financial and other reforms which had to be taken in order to pave the way for the attainment of these goals. It is supercilious, however, to infer that the ordinary revolutionary of the South was incapable of comprehending or was completely uninterested in reforms which provided for the democratization of the nation's political life, for greater independence from foreign influences, for more equitable distribution of wealth and for higher levels of living. Democratic political and social reforms and greater independence from foreign control would assure the peasant the free exploitation of his parcel of land. The peasant had acquired this understanding of his problems and the means to solve them through his experiences in everyday life. His daily struggle, at first pacific and later armed, against political imposition, economic exploitation, and armed repression had given him a fundamental grasp of underlying social realities which individuals from more socially privileged environments might well have envied.

The acceptance of Marxist leadership by peasant movements in Asia, Africa and Latin America and the cooperation of the peasants in China and North Vietnam, for example, in the construction of a socialist order should make one wary of overly-simplistic and supercilious interpretations of "the peasant mentality." The peasant's understanding of Marxist concepts may well not equal that of their leaders, but the iron determination of their struggles as well as the cooperation they lend to the task of constructing socialism in their nations once victory is achieved would seem to indicate that these peasants have at least a good general grasp of the goals which they seek.

The *zapatista* military operations were more limited in scope than those of the *villistas* or *carrancistas* primarily because the Army of the South suffered a chronic shortage of arms and ammunition. The *villistas* were able to supply themselves by railroad through Ciudad Juárez and the *carrancistas* received supplies by sea through Vera Cruz. The former had the cattle and cotton of Chihuahua and Coahuila to finance their purchases of arms and the latter the oil of Tampico and Vera Cruz. The revolutionaries of the South had no such ready access to funds or to foreign arms merchants. The Army of the South, constantly confronted with better equipped forces, had to adopt the cautious, hit and run tactics of guerrilla warfare. In accordance with the exigencies of that type of warfare, Zapata and his men engaged in large-scale battles, such as those of Cuautla, Cuernavaca and Puebla, only when they were reasonably certain of victory. Inadequate armaments, therefore, not their supposed circumscribed peasant outlook, forced this guerrilla style of warfare upon the men of the South. Zapata was too good a strategist to risk losing everything in a single battle with well equipped troops.

In spite of their limited armaments, the *zapatistas* carried on military operations in an extensive area of central and southern Mexico, including the states of Morelos, Guerrero, Puebla, Oaxaca, Tlaxcala, Hidalgo and México. In the South, their operations extended as far as the Isthmus of Tehuantepec and the western part of the state of Chiapas.[8] Thus, in the latter part of 1915, Zapata sent General Rafael Cal y Mayor and his men to operate in the latter's native Chiapas where the *zapatista* general maintained the struggle against the *carrancistas* and *felicistas* (followers of Felix Díaz, nephew of Porfirio Díaz) until Obregón overthrew the Carranza government in 1920.[9] In the North, a small band of *zapatistas* fought in the states of Nuevo León and Tamaulipas in 1918 in order to stimulate sentiments of rebellion against Carranza's regime in these states.[10] In short, the *zapatistas* operated wherever their strength permitted them, thereby further belying the claim that they could not see beyond the local interests of Morelos.

According to the historian, Robert Quirk, the Conventionists could have won a decisive victory if they had attacked the Constitutionalists in Veracruz in December 1914. That the Conventionists did not attack, continues this author, was due in part to the fact that the *zapatistas* "had no real concern for capturing Veracruz or even for defeating the First Chief." Rather, according to Quirk, the *zapatistas* were concerned only with their homeland, Morelos; their limited peasant mentality could conceive of nothing better to do after they had taken Puebla from the Constitutionlists in December 1914 than to return home *en masse* to their fields, thereby destroying the offensive potentiality of the Army of the South. Quirk admits that serious tactical considerations entered into Villa's decision not to move his Division of the North on Veracruz but claims, nevertheless, that Villa was stayed principally by his concern for his native countryside which caused him to be unduly alarmed over the threat which Constitutionalist troops posed to Torreón.[11] This same author provides information which tends to contradict his allegations.

In their conversations at Xochimilco early in December 1914, Villa and Zapata had agreed to attack the Constitutionalists in Veracruz. Zapata was to take Puebla and Villa was to advance on Veracruz by way of Apizaco. Zapata did not indicate the slightest reluctance to fulfill the plan. On the contrary, he complained of a chronic shortage of arms and ammunition and requested Villa to supply him with heavy artillery. This is hardly the attitude of the commander of an army which is about to disintegrate to plant corn in its homeland. Zapata fulfilled his part of the plan, taking Puebla from the Constitutionalists on December 15. Villa, however, decided that the threat posed by Constitutionalist armies in his rear, especially in Michoacán and Coahuila, was too great to risk carrying out the planned attack on Veracruz.

Villa's decision was probably well taken. Although the *carrancistas* had suffered some defections, the Constitutionalist army in Veracruz was by no means a weak or disorganized force awaiting Villa's *coup de grace* as Quirk implies. On the contrary, the army in Veracruz had never suffered defeat and it had one of the ablest generals of the revolution as its commander, Álvaro Obregón. It was this army which four months later shattered Villa's Division of the North at Celaya. Furthermore, if Villa had moved on Veracruz it is fairly certain that the Constitutionalist troops in his rear would have cut off his supply lines to the north and also might well have attacked him from behind, trapping his forces in Veracruz in the tropical regions between the mountains and the sea. In regard to the relative strength of the contending armies, it is well to remember that Villa's forces were drawn largely from the states of Chihuahua, Durango and Zacatecas; much of the remainder of northern Mexico was Constitutionalist. Similarly, although *zapatista* bands operated widely, the Army of the South drew its strength largely from a relatively few states in central and south-central Mexico; the Constitutionalists predominated elsewhere. Also, although Zapata's forces were sizeable, their fire power did not match their numbers. In short, if the Convention forces had attacked Veracruz, they might well have suffered a defeat of similar proportions to that which Villa sustained at Celaya in April 1915 and perhaps with the additional consequence that the Army of the South would also have been destroyed as an effective military force.

It would be absurd, of course, to suggest that the *zapatistas* alone should have attempted what the well-armed Division of the North feared to do. Zapata was too good a strategist to risk losing his army in a suicidal adventure. It was tactical considerations, therefore, which stayed the men of the South and not a sudden seizure of monomaniacal desire to sniff freshly turned earth. As mentioned previously, in order to feed the troops and the villagers, the Army of the South regularly alternated its men between three-month periods of active service and of agricultural labors in the villages. The objective of this system was to maintain in the field a permanent army composed largely of peasants without at the same time disrupting the economic life of the peasant villages.

Zapata's army remained intact and, in spite of its limited armament, was quite active against the Constitutionalists after the battle of Puebla, as it had been before. Thus, from October to December 1914, the *zapatistas* took the following towns in Puebla from the enemy forces (although they subsequently evacuated some of these places shortly after taking them): Todos Santos Almolonga on October 8; Tehuacán on October 22; Chietla on November 9; San Martín Texmolucan on November 18 and again on December 11; Matamoros Izúcar at the end of November; and Cholula on December 13.[12] After taking Puebla on December 15, the *zapatistas* advanced on Tehuacán (which is on the route to Vera Cruz) with 5,000 men, but were defeated in Tecamachalco toward the end of December. As mentioned previously, the Constitutionalists recaptured Puebla from the poorly equipped Army of the South in January 1915.

After Obregón's forces entered Mexico City toward the end of January 1915, the Army of the South placed the capital under such heavy attack that, in the words of Obregón, "Mexico could consider itself in a state of siege." Obregón noted at first a lack of unity of command among the attackers, but spoke later of generalized attacks all along the line of defense, which placed the defenders in such straits that guards from the Constitutionalist general headquarters and soldiers from the *Comandancia Militar de la Plaza* (the military authority in the Capital) had to be rushed to the front as reinforcements. According to Obregón, the men of the South suffered heavy losses but he also admitted that his forces suffered an average of 60 men killed or wounded daily. The Constitutionalist troops were unable to operate outside the Capital or even to extend their lines to nearby Xochimilco where the plant which supplied water to the Capital was located. The Constitutionalists were able to keep railroad communications with Vera Cruz open, but only by reason of constant efforts. Obregón evacuated Mexico City in March 1915 with few losses due, according to Obregón, to the "torpidness of the enemy" and to the efficiency with which the evacuation was undertaken.[13] In the spring of 1915, the *zapatistas* began to operate in the state of Vera Cruz.

In the summer of 1915, the southern revolutionaries were forced to abandon Mexico City to forces under the command of the *carrancista* general, Pablo González. The problem of munitions was paramount in the *zapatista* defeat. Thus, Octavio Paz, who makes the men of the South's arms and munitions problems clear in his work, notes that the *zapatistas* had to abandon excellent strategic positions during their defense of the city because of lack of munitions.[14] The armed strength of the Constitutionalists was too great for the defenders.

The above details may indicate that Zapata's forces could well have been better organized—the *zapatistas* never achieved the degree of organization and discipline of contemporary guerrilla forces such as those in South Vietnam—but they also demonstrate that the revolutionaries of the South were quite active in their struggle with Carranza's forces. I think it safe to assume that it was the military power of the well armed *carrancistas* which limited the successes of the relatively poorly armed *zapatistas* and not the latter's supposed lack of interest in operating beyond the limits of their *patria chica*.

As with "Indianism," so with socialism; the material presented in this work does not reveal a genuine socialist bias to Zapata's movement. References to the exploitation of the proletariat or criticisms of capitalist monopolists and of foreign imperialism are not incompatible with a radical petty-bourgeois philosophy. Zapata's movement, to be sure, contained an element of collectivism in that it advocated granting *ejidos* to villages and recommended the formation of consumers' and producers' cooperatives in the countryside. It must be remembered that the *ejido* was the Mexican village's traditional form of land tenure and that the land, although possessed collectively by the village, was divided in parcels among the families of the village. The formation of consumers' and producers' cooperatives would have collectivized labor on the *ejidos* to a degree but, as we have noted, the *zapatistas* contemplated that the peasant would retain possession of his individual parcel. The formation of these cooperatives might have served as an intermediary step in the organization of genuine agricultural cooperatives in the Mexican countryside. On the other hand, they might have served, at least for a time, to prevent the formation of genuine cooperatives and state farms, which appears to be the case with producers' and consumers' cooperatives in western Europe.

Furthermore, the *zapatistas* also advocated the creation of small, individual properties. As we have noted, the *zapatista* measures of agrarian reform, if implemented, would have left properties in private hands, of sufficient size to permit the flourishing of a capitalist agriculture in Mexico. Also, although the Plan of Ayala provided for the nationalization of the properties of enemies of the revolution, the urban properties expropriated under this provision were sold and the proceeds used to found agricultural credit banks, and the rural properties were distributed among the peasants.

One author claims that Zapata's delegates and others made "socialist allusions" and that "echoes" of Marx and Kropotkin were heard at the Aguascalientes Convention.[15] This may well have been the case. However, the extensive quotations from

major speeches delivered at the Convention which I have examined[16] do not really reveal any sound socialist or anarchist
bias. These "allusions" and "echoes" must have been no more
than just that.

In his work previously cited, Díaz Soto y Gama reproduced an
account which Zapata's former private secretary, Serafín M.
Robles, gave in 1947 concerning Zapata's reaction to certain
individuals who tried to get him to accept "communist" ideas.
According to Robles, Zapata told these individuals that he had
listened "with the greatest interest" to their explanations of
communism and had read the books they had given him. These
ideas, declared Zapata, seemed to him "good and humane" but
he felt that it was impractical to attempt to implement them right
away; that was a task for future generations. For now, continued
Zapata, the implementation of the Plan of Ayala would "be sufficient to procure not only the economic improvement of the rural
class, but also the well-being of all the country and city workers,
for progress will occur in agriculture, cattle raising, mining, industry and commerce." Zapata added that if, after many years of
struggle, the people still have not been able to implement the
precepts of the Plan of Ayala, much less could they be expected
to set for themselves other and more difficult goals. Zapata
concluded, according to Robles, by declaring that he would not
change "a single comma" in the Plan of Ayala. "If what is said
therein is fulfilled," added Zapata, "I am sure that the happiness
of the people will be realized."[17]

Zapata made some statements which seemingly would indicate
a socialist bias to his thinking in a letter dated February 14,
1918, which he directed to General Jenaro Amezcua in Havana,
Cuba. (Zapata had sent General Amezcua on an international
mission to propagandize the *zapatista* cause.) At one point
in the letter, Zapata declared:

"Much would we gain, much would human justice gain, if all
the people of our America and all the nations of old Europe
should understand that the cause of revolutionary Mexico and the
cause of Russia, the unredeemed, are and represent the cause of

humanity, the supreme interest of all oppressed people. Here, as there, there are great lords, inhuman, greedy and cruel, who from fathers to sons have been exploiting great masses of peasants to the point of torture. And here, as there, the enslaved men, the men with sleeping consciences, begin to awake, to shake themselves, to agitate and to castigate.

"Mr. Wilson, the President of the United States, was right to render homage on a recent occasion to the Russian Revolution, qualifying it as a noble effort to attain freedom. One can only wish in this respect that [people] would remember and take well into account the visible analogy, the marked paralellism, or, better said, the absolute parity which exists between that movement and Mexico's agrarian revolution. The one and the other are directed against what Leon Tolstoy would call the great crime against the infamous usurpation of the land which, being the property of everyone, as water and air, has been monopolized by a few powerful individuals supported by the force of armies and the iniquity of the law.

"It is not strange, for this reason, that the proletariat of the world applauds and admires the Russian Revolution in the same manner as it will lend its complete adhesion, sympathy and support to the Mexican Revolution once it fully comprehends its objectives."[18]

The letter went on to request General Amezcua to make every effort to expound the cause of the Mexican Revolution in the labor confederations of Europe and America. Zapata noted that the workers and peasants must unite their forces if either one or the other is to gain its emancipation. Otherwise, as occurred in Mexico, the bourgeoisie may set these classes against one another, thereby frustrating the hopes of both.

It is obvious from his comments that Zapata was attracted principally by the agrarian features of the Russian Revolution. His claim of "absolute parity" between the Russian and Mexican revolutions would lead one to judge that he did not recognize the distinctive proletarian, socialist character of the former. Certainly, one cannot say on the basis of this letter that

Zapata had adopted a socialist, much less a Marxist-socialist position. Nevertheless, one can speculate on the basis of Zapata's praise of the Russian Revolution, his recognition of the necessity for united action by the workers and peasants, and his hostility toward the bourgeoisie that Zapata and his peasant followers may have accepted the leadership of a Marxist political party if one had existed in Mexico. Such a party would have had to be strong and to possess an intelligent appreciation of the strategy and tactics appropriate to Mexican reality. At the same time, such a party would probably have had to capture the leadership of the revolution of the South from its inception, before it formed a well-defined, petty-bourgeois ideology. Once the revolution of the South had acquired a definite ideological orientation, it is questionable whether it would have exchanged its ideology for another, as Zapata's response to the individuals who tried to influence him with socialist ideas would seem to indicate.

Zapata's letter to Amezcua raises the tantalizing subject of the influence of the Russian Revolution upon Zapata's thinking. I have, however, found no direct documentary evidence of that influence other than this letter. It is, nevertheless, worthwhile to point out that although Zapata stressed the importance of worker demands and of attracting the workers to his cause throughout the revolution, his statements in 1918 on the need for worker-peasant unity stand out for their force and clarity. It may not be unwarranted to speculate, therefore, that Zapata's thinking on this matter was influenced, at least to the extent of reinforcing and clarifying his own thoughts on the subject, by knowledge of the importance of the unity of these forces in the Russian Revolution. The Russian experience, it may be added, did have considerable impact upon certain of Mexico's radical elements and contributed directly to the formation of the Mexican Communist Party in 1919.

One may speculate that Zapata, frustrated in his attempts to achieve genuine emancipation of the peasantry, perhaps was at least veering toward a more radical position. He was perhaps close to recognizing that only a proletarian revolution and the construction of a socialist civilization in Mexico could lay the bases for the genuine emancipation of the Mexican workers and peasants. Apart from all speculation, Zapata's comments in his letter to Amezcua indicate the genuineness of his revolutionary posture.

Some critics of the *zapatistas* during the revolution alleged that the revolutionaries of the South were anarchists.[19] Enrique and Ricardo Flores Magón had formed a small anarchist group early in the Mexican Revolution. Their manifesto of September 23, 1911, called for the immediate destruction of the state, the expropriation of the propertied classes and the reconstitution of society on the basis of voluntary organizations which would produce communally and share products according to need.[20] The exact extent of the influence of the *magonistas* upon the revolution of the South is difficult to determine. It is probable that the *zapatistas* were acquainted with the *magonista* newspaper, the *Regeneración*.[21]

The journalist, Paulino Martínez, who headed the *zapatista* delegation to the Aguascalientes Convention, published a pamphlet shortly before he joined the *zapatistas* in 1914 in which he claimed that the people of Mexico had a natural right to possess enough land to maintain themselves and, consequently, called upon the people to take possession of the land spontaneously and to organize self-managed "Communal Agricultural Colonies." The land and instruments of labor in these colonies were to be owned in common. The industrial and commercial activities of the colony were to be carried on "by means of the cooperative system or mutual exchange of products, avoiding at all times the exploitation of man by man." It is not clear whether Martínez contemplated communal or individual exploitation of the land in these colonies, but it is probable that he thought in terms of the latter. Thus, at one point in the pamphlet Martínez claimed: "Give every Mexican his piece of land so that he may cultivate it and build his home [construct experimental farm schools throughout Mexico], and thereby we will have consummated a prodigy." Since these concepts bear some resemblance to those expressed by Ricardo Flores Magón in regard to the land question in Mexico and also since, like Flores Magón, Martínez denounced clericalism, militarism and plutocracy as the principal enemies of the Mexican people, we may speculate that Martínez had been influenced by the former's writings. Martínez, however, expressly denied that his concepts were anarchistic. Indeed, his ideas are quite compatible with the semi-communal *ejido* and worker's cooperative movements of revolutionary and post-revolutionary Mexico. Also, Martínez merely wished to democratize the national government, not eliminate it.[22]

Several others of the petty-bourgeois intellectuals associated with the *zapatistas* were influenced by anarchist concepts, although perhaps none could properly have been called an anarchist. Díaz Soto y Gama attended reunions and spoke before meetings called by the *Casa del Obrero Mundial* before he joined the *zapatistas*.[23] One former member of the *Casa* had claimed that Díaz Soto y Gama professed a Tolstoyian form of anarchism during his association with the *Casa*.[24] The *Casa* was a working class organization formed in Mexico City in 1912 by Spanish anarchists; a mixture of anarchist and socialist ideas prevailed among its members. In his work, *La Revolución Agraria del Sur y Emiliano Zapata, su Caudillo,* Díaz Soto y Gama admitted the influence upon him and others of anarchist doctrines when, referring to the *zapatista* delegates in the Convention government, he stated that: "Those of us who were at the head of the delegation from the South (Santiago Orozco, Luís Mendez, Otilio Montaño and this writer) found ourselves saturated with readings and impressions concerning the French Revolution and strongly impressed also, with the exception of Montaño, by the doctrines derived from the anarchistic concepts of Kropotkin, Reclus, Malatesta, and other theoreticians of anarchism." Later in his work, Díaz Soto y Gama takes pains to indicate that Zapata was neither an anarchist nor a "communist."[25]

Although anarchist concepts undoubtedly influenced some revolutionaries of the South, nevertheless, the exposition given previously of the ideas and practical activities of the *zapatista* would lead to the conclusion that these ideas did not penetrate the revolution of the South sufficiently to warrant designating that movement as "anarchist." Thus, the men of the South wished to democratize the state, not eliminate it, and although they sought to distribute property widely, they also would have left sufficient lands in private hands to permit a bourgeois agriculture to flourish in Mexico. Furthermore, although the *zapatistas* proposed to forbid the formation of monopolies, to protect and encourage small owners and to defend the rights of the proletariat, they also contemplated that capitalist property relationships would continue to prevail in industry, finance and commerce.

Indeed, rather than anarchism *per se*, the intellectuals associated with the *zapatistas* demonstrated an agrarian oriented, petty-bourgeois romanticism similar to that of Rousseau and Jefferson. The intellectuals gave an example of their romanticism in an article published in the *zapatista* organ, *El Sur,* on January 1, 1918. The anonymous author contrasted what he considered to be the purely political revolution of the *carrancistas* with the economic revolution which the men of the South were carrying out in practice by dividing lands among the peasants. This division of the latifundias laid the foundations for the freedom of the peasant and at the same time offered the city worker, "as a sure means to free himself from capitalist exploitation, fecund farming lands, land of generous fruit, in order to go there to the source of wealth and life when the slavery of the workshop weighs down too much and there arises the desire to breath freedom deeply far from the unhealthy atmosphere of the city and under the protective dome of the heavens."

The article continued: "'You philosophers are very humorous,' Jean Jacque Rousseau used to say, 'because you consider city dwellers the only ones to whom you have duties to fulfill. Where one learns to love and to be useful to humanity is in the countryside; in the cities one learns to despise it.' "[26]

Anarchism has its origins in an extreme form of petty-bourgeois liberalism. One must be careful, therefore, not to confuse these two social philosophies and mistake expressions of hostility toward the dictatorial state for a desire to eliminate the state immediately, or interpret criticisms of monopolies and the big bourgeoisie as a desire to destroy capitalist property relationships. In accordance with such interpretations, Jefferson and Tom Paine were anarchists!

There remains for us to consider the concept of Mexico's distinguished historian and economist, Jesús Silva Herzog, that the Mexican Revolution was anti-bourgeois in character.[27] Silva Herzog claims the revolution was especially anti-bourgeois in the central part of Mexico—that is, where the *zapatistas* operated. We may say on the basis of the examination we have made of its ideas and actions that the revolution of the South was anti-bourgeois only in the sense that it was radical petty-bourgeois. In this sense, strong anti-bourgeois currents existed also in the French and American Revolutions. The *zapatistas* were not anti-bourgeois, however, in the sense that they wished to destroy bourgeois property relationships—surely the only test of a genuine anti-bourgeois attitude. It was feudal, not bourgeois, social relationships which the men of the South sought to destroy. The *zapatista* proposals which mentioned the interests of the working class looked to the *improvement* of the worker's conditions *within* the framework of capitalist property relationships by such means as guaranteeing workers the right to organize and to strike, providing for shorter hours of labor, and so forth. In short, as noted above, although the *zapatistas* sought to protect and promote the interests of small proprietors, they also envisioned that bourgeois property relationships would continue to prevail in industry, commerce and finance. The Convention's agrarian law of October 26, 1915, left substantial quantities of lands in the hands of private owners, who inevitably would form a rural bourgeoisie. Finally, Zapata left most of the sugar mills in Morelos in private hands.

In short, the reforms for which the *zapatistas* struggled—the wide distribution of landed property throughout Mexico, the realization of a democratic, parliamentary form of government, the guaranteeing of rights to labor within a capitalist framework of property relationships, the restriction of imperialist penetration into Mexico—would create an independent, liberal-bourgeois Mexico in which, in contrast to the 19th-century liberal ideal, the state would play an active role in guaranteeing the rights of certain social classes and in limiting the influence of foreign imperialism upon the nation.

CHAPTER V

Revolutionary Tactics

We tend our arms to everyone except the enemies of the popular cause. — Emiliano Zapata

Why were the *zapatistas* not more successful in their efforts? The men of the South did not achieve victory in the revolution largely because they failed to attract widespread support from social classes other than the peasantry, and they were unable even to unify the entire Mexican peasantry under their leadership. The failure of the *zapatistas* to attract widespread support was not due to lack of effort on their part to construct a broad base for their movement. Zapata did not wish to rely solely upon the support of the peasants in order to achieve victory. Rather, and especially in the years from 1915 onward, he attempted to form a broad, national front of all the anti-feudal, anti-imperialist and democratic-bourgeois elements in Mexico.

We saw in Chapter III that Zapata offered guarantees to many social groups and classes and called upon them for support. Zapata's interest in the political plan issued by a revolutionary group of workers and intellectuals in Mexico City in 1911 revealed his desire even at this early date to attract the support of radical middle class and urban working class elements. As we noted, several members of this group joined Zapata's movement. The Program of Politico-Social Reforms which the Convention government issued in Cuernavaca in 1916 proposed reforms in benefit of various social classes and indicated thereby a desire on the part of the *zapatistas* to enlist the support of the industrial workers and of radical elements among the petty bourgeoisie, the bourgeoisie, and the intellectuals.

Zapata's attempt to form a national, revolutionary front is evident especially in the Manifesto to the Mexican People which he issued on January 20, 1917. In this manifesto he pointed out that the revolution offered reforms and guarantees to workers, peasants, merchants, industrialists and bankers and went on to offer those who had remained neutral in the revolutionary struggles a "cordial invitation" to cooperate in the forthcoming political, economic and social reconstruction of Mexico. The breadth of the Zapata appeal was evident in his offer to "tender our arms to everyone except the enemies of the popular cause, except the unrepentant reactionaries, the incorrigible, indomitable and stubborn obstructionists."[1]

Zapata issued a decree (not previously referred to in this work) on March 1, 1917, which granted amnesty to all officers and troops of the Constitutionalist army who put aside their arms and presented themselves before one of the chiefs of the Liberator Army before May 31, 1917.[2] The decree was issued in view of the fact, according to Zapata, that many *carrancistas* were demoralized over recent *zapatista* victories and were beginning to surrender in groups of 50 to 100 men. Zapata hoped to weaken the enemy by taking men from him.[3]

In his Manifesto to the People of April 20, 1917, Zapata declared: "The nation demands a serene and reposed government which gives guarantees to all and does not exclude any sound element capable of lending services to the revolution and to society. Therefore, we will find room in our ranks for all those who in good faith pretend to work with us."[4]

As a final example we may note Zapata's manifesto of February 27, 1918, in which he denounced the unpopular, counter-revolutionary character of the Carranza regime and called for unity among all the progressive forces in Mexico to overthrow Carranza. Zapata declared: "'Revolutionary unification through the elimination of Carranza,' such is the common aspiration of all true revolutionaries."[5]

In addition to domestic support, the *zapatistas* sought diplomatic support from foreign nations. Thus, Zapata wrote a letter to Woodrow Wilson in August 1914, explaining the history of the revolution and the motives and objectives of his movement, and he gave a cordial reception to Wilson's special representative in Mexico, Duval West. An Exposition to the Mexican People and to the Diplomatic Corps issued in October, 1916, announced to the foreign diplomats that the revolution of the South did not recognize Carranza's authority and declared null and void all the transactions of the latter's regime. The intention of the Exposition was obviously to undermine the authority of the Constitutionalist government and to augment the international prestige of his movement. Zapata, or, more precisely, the Convention government in Cuernavaca, sent General Amezcua and Octavio Paz abroad in 1916, the former to Havana, Cuba, and the latter to the United States, to act as propagandists for the revolutionary movement against Carranza. The *zapatista* agents were to explain to the world the nature and objectives of the revolutionary movement and thereby gain sympathy for the revolutionaires, counteract *carrancista* propaganda, and undermine international confidence in the Carranza regime.[6] In their relations with foreign governments, the *zapatistas* never offered to make concessions harmful to Mexico's national interests in return for diplomatic support, nor did the Liberator Army of the South ever receive arms and munitions from abroad.

Zapata manifested his desire for the support of the Mexican workers on numerous occasions. As we have seen, the manifestos and other documents of the *zapatistas* generally mentioned the problems of labor and, after the Constitutionalists took control of the national government, roundly criticized the anti-labor policies of the Carranza regime. Although the *zapatista* documents denounced capitalists and the exploitative character of the capital-labor relationship, they did not propose the socialization of industry. Rather, they called for the genuine realization in practice of rights guaranteed to labor within the capitalist system, such as the right to organize, strike and boycott.

In a letter to General Amezcua dated February 14, 1918, quoted from previously, Zapata revealed his desire to unify the workers and peasants to overthrow the Carranza regime. At the same time, his remarks indicated his failure to achieve this objective.

"It is necessary not to forget that in virtue of, and for the end of, the solidarity of the proletariat, the emancipation of the worker cannot be achieved if the liberation of the peasant is not realized at the same time. If this does not happen, the bourgeoisie could make these two forces confront one another and take advantage, for example, of the ignorance of the peasants to combat and check the just impulses of the city workers; in the same manner, that if the need arose, it could utilize the workers of little consciousness and set them against their brothers in the countryside. Francisco Madero at first and Venustiano Carranza lately have done this in Mexico, although here the workers have parted from their error and understand now perfectly well that they were victims of *carrancista* perfidy."[7]

The men of the South summoned the support of the workers in an article published in *El Sur* on March 15, 1918. The article called upon all workers—miners, railroaders, stevedores and factory hands, in every part of the republic, in Puebla and Monterrey, in Orizaba and León, in Guadalajara and Pachuca, in Cananea and Parral—to join with the peasants to overthrow the Carranza regime. The article claimed that Carranza's was a bourgeois regime allied with the exploiters of labor. Carranza accepted the armed support of the workers when it was convenient for him to do so; later he broke strikes, imprisoned labor leaders and closed the *Casa del Obrero Mundial*. The article went on to claim that the workers, who demanded shorter hours and higher wages, and the peasants, who fought to achieve the distribution of lands, were struggling to achieve the same goal of economic liberty. The workers sought to attain their ends through the relatively peaceful actions of their labor unions; the peasants, more tyrannized than the workers, could free themselves only by means of armed revolution. The article claimed that victory was near over *carrancismo*, "the most perfidious of the disguises with which the bourgeoisie has clothed itself in our country" and called upon the workers to accelerate that victory by joining with the *zapatistas*. The article concluded: "May the calloused hands of the countryside and the calloused hands of the workshop unite in a fraternal salute of concord because, in truth, if the workers are united we are invincible, we are the force and we are the right; we are the tomorrow! Health, brother worker, health, your friend the peasant awaits you!"[8]

In a letter to Obregón in August 1918, Zapata expressed quite clearly not only his desire to unite the Mexican workers and peasants but also the frustration of his efforts to achieve that goal. He declared that agrarian radicalism and city worker radicalism should unite to achieve "political freedom and worker redemption," and went on to say:

"That the revolution of the country represents the interest of the majority and that of the towns points out the procedure for the rectification and dignifying of the Mexican Indian, no one can deny. It is also beyond question that the city revolution is founded upon powerful agents of progress, in inevitable connection with which are the problems of bettering the status of the depressed working classes. The fundamental error...in all our action since 1915 consists in our two forces having remained divided and in conflict and, rather than gravitating together, in detracting from each other.

"Here is the explanation for our not having been able to establish peace in our country in spite of the complete triumph over reaction as represented by Huerta.... Why not unify the Revolution?... Why not accomplish this patriotic act of brotherhood and accord if it will serve to eliminate the spurious element of personalism?"[9]

The response of Mexico's social classes to Zapata's plea for unity was negative. Zapata's support was limited largely to a portion of the peasantry and to a limited number of students and intellectuals from the urban centers. The *zapatista* general, Jenaro Amezcua, admitted as much in an interview which he granted in Havana to the Cuban newspaper, *El Mundo*, in 1917.

Amezcua declared that: "These forces united, that of the peasant determined to fight to the last and that of the studious and ideal loving youth, must be decisive in the problem stated."[10] The youthful general revealed in his statement that his conception of revolutionary strategy was not the equal of Zapata's, because whereas the latter sought to form a broad union of Mexico's social classes in order to achieve victory, Amezcua thought the support of young people and peasants was sufficient to that end.

The revolution of the South failed to attract substantial support from the urban working class, although it did receive support in individual cases.[11] The *Casa del Obrero Mundial* which, as noted previously, was a working class organization formed in 1912 by Spanish anarchists, formed six "red battalions" in 1915 which fought under the command of *carrancista* generals. (In previous years, however, some individuals associated with the *Casa*, such as Díaz Soto y Gama, had joined Zapata's movement.) Carranza ordered these battalions disbanded after the *villistas* were defeated.[12] In addition, Carranza took severe measures to suppress strikes in the summer of 1916 and he closed the *Casa*. The Mexican workers became more radical as a consequence of these measures, but they did not, in general, move to Marxist-socialist positions, nor did they ally themselves with the revolution of the South.[13]

The revolutionaries of the South attracted only limited support from the urban petty bourgeois and the bourgeoisie, although they were able to draw a number of middle class intellectuals to their ranks, including individuals as capable as Martínez, Díaz Soto y Gama, and Paz. Zapata's movement, nevertheless, could well have made use of greater support from the urban centers. In a conversation held in Xochimilco in December 1914, Villa and Zapata revealed the problems caused them by their failure to attract substantial support from the cities. The conversation was recorded in shorthand.

Both revolutionary leaders recognized the incapacity of many of their followers to fill high government posts, and both expressed concern over the problem of finding men who could be entrusted with such vital appointments. At one point Villa claimed: "I do not need public positions because I don't know how to contend with them. Let's see where those people are [who can]. Just entrust them and they'll give trouble." Zapata responded: "Because of this I advise all my friends to be very careful, because if not, the machete will fall." Zapata added, however, that he did not think they would be deceived by the intellectuals; that he had been carefully nurturing a group for the future.[14]

The men of the South were not unique in their failure to attract substantial support from the urban petty bourgeoisie and bourgeoisie, including petty-bourgeois intellectuals. The failure of the latter to participate in the armed struggles of the revolution was notorious. With some notable exceptions, Mexican intellectuals during the revolution at best merely hoped passively for the victory of one or another of the revolutionary factions. At worst, they were disinterested spectators or collaborationists with the reactionary elements. Those relatively few intellectuals who did participate in the revolution were subordinated to the military chieftains.[15]

The men of the South might well have prevailed against their foes without support from the urban centers if they had been able to unite the entire peasantry under their leadership. Such a union occurred in part when the *villistas* and *zapatistas* united their forces in the Convention. Even with this union, however, the peasantry remained substantially divided. Zapata's movement centered principally in the states of Morelos, Guerrero, Puebla, México, Tlaxcala, and Hidalgo, although he had pockets of strength in Vera Cruz, Oaxaca and even Chiapas. Similarly, although Villa drew his men from a number of states in northern Mexico, the bulk of his forces were from Chihuahua, Durango and Zacatecas. The peasantry in much of the remainder of the country, in so far as it participated in the armed struggles, followed the Constitutionalist banner. Peasant was set against peasant in the clashes between the Constitutionalists and the Conventionists.

Why were the *zapatistas* not more successful in attracting allies to their cause? In seeking an answer to this question, it would be well at the outset to consider whether or not the social reform program of the revolution of the South contained any proposals which, if implemented, would have in any way impeded Mexico's social progress, and therefore have alienated the potential support of some individuals or social classes. In this respect we may consider the *zapatista* proposals for land reform and their attitude toward the intervention of the state in the economy.

As mentioned previously, the distribution of land among many small holders may have undesired consequences when undertaken in the 20th century because developments in technology have, in many cases, made small units of production inefficient. Nevertheless, the revolutionary movement had to destroy the semi-feudal mode of production in Mexico and to undermine the political power of the large landowners in order to lay the political and economic bases for implementing a modern program of development in Mexico. The only practical way for the revolutionary movement to accomplish these objectives, as previously indicated, was to distribute land widely among the peasants.

The distribution of lands undertaken during the regime of Lázaro Cárdenas in the 1930s stimulated Mexico's economic and human development, and we may speculate that the stimulus would have been much greater if these reforms had been implemented two decades earlier. Furthermore, the *zapatistas* recognized the economic inefficiency of the small parcel and proposed to create consumers' and producers' cooperatives in order to make the peasant's labor more productive. In addition, the limits which they set to the amount of land which private individuals could hold were ample enough to permit a capitalist agriculture to develop and flourish in Mexico.

As noted previously, the *zapatistas* in their Program of Politico-Social Reforms, issued in 1916, called for somewhat less intervention by the state in the economy than others thought necessary in order to promote Mexico's development. Their tendency, however, was to support state intervention where essential (as, for example, in providing guarantees for the work-ers, in overseeing the distribution of land, in regulating the ex-ploitation of Mexico's natural resources by foreigners, in ensuring the revolutionary character of the political administrations in the various states). The *zapatista* Program and the Constitution of 1917 are similar in spirit; the orientation of both documents is anti-feudal, bourgeois-democratic and anti-imperialist. In short, implementation of the *zapatista* program of social reforms would not have produced undesirable consequences for Mexico's development. Hence, we must look elsewhere for the answer to the question posed above as to why Zapata's movement did not have greater success in attracting allies.

Why did not the urban workers and the urban petty-bourgeoisie and bourgeoisie unite with the *zapatistas*? The peasantry on the one hand and, on the other, the urban bourgeoisie and petty-bourgeoisie had conflicting interests. It was in the interests of the latter that the prices of food and raw materials from the countryside be low and that the prices paid in the countryside for industrial products be relatively high. The peasant's interest, of course, was the reverse. Since a significant part of working class income was spent on food, cheap food supplies strengthened the bargaining position of the capitalists in their efforts to keep wages down. Similarly, the less capitalists had to pay for agricul-tural raw materials, the greater their profit margins and the stronger their competitive position in the national and inter-national markets. Merchants and moneylenders prospered to the degree that the peasant was unable to defend himself against poor terms of exchange and high interest rates. Capitalists, therefore, had a vested interest in a divided and weak peasantry. Zapata's movement meant unity and strength; hence it had to be destroyed.

The bourgeoisie, it is worth emphasizing, was not necessarily hostile to agrarian reform. It had to break the semi-feudal mode of production in Mexico in order to make possible the formation of internal markets for the sale of products and the purchase of raw materials and labor power; the formation of these commodity markets was an essential prerequisite for, or had to be coincident with, the development of capitalist enterprises. The destruction of the semi-feudal hacienda was a political imperative also; only by destroying the economic power of the large landowners could the bourgeoisie be secure in its control of the state power. What was essential to the bourgeoisie, however, was to destroy the revolutionary unity and independence of the peasantry and, we might add, to prevent the revolutionary unity of the working class.

As for the proletariat, unless it rejected the bourgeois system of human relationships for a socialist one, it would tend to unite with the bourgeoisie rather than with the peasantry. The proletariat also had an interest in cheap food supplies and, in so far as industry developed and prospered, proletarians might expect some improvement in their living conditions.

Only a radicalized, socialist-oriented proletariat might have joined with the peasantry instead of following the lead of the nascent bourgeoisie. Such a peasant-worker union occurred in the Russian Revolution of 1917. In that case, though, the peasantry was also influenced by socialist ideas and, more important, the proletariat was guided by a Marxist political party. The Russian peasantry accepted the leadership of the Marxist-led proletariat and acquiesced in the reorganization of society under the direction of representatives of that class. No counterpart to the Bolsheviks (or even to the Mensheviks) existed in Mexico. The only organized radical influence was that of the anarchists, represented by Ricardo Flores Magón and his small group of followers and by the *Casa del Obrero Mundial,* in which a mixture of anarchist and socialist ideas prevailed. As we have seen, the *Casa,* with some individual exceptions, supported the *carrancistas.* It was probably the undeveloped character of the Mexican proletariat as a social class in comparison to its counterpart in Russian society which accounted for the former's lack of ideological preparation. Hence, considering the limited ideological preparation of the Mexican proletariat, it is probable that the peasants, due to their numbers and their armed strength, would have dominated any union with the workers.[16]

As we have noted, the *zapatistas* might have been able to triumph even without the support of urban elements if they had been able to unite the entire peasantry behind them. Why were they unable to do so?

Several aspects of Mexican national life made it difficult for the peasants to unify. The influence of *caudillismo* was perhaps the most important source of division among the peasants. Autocracy and servility prevailed in Mexican social relationships; petty autocrats or caudillos found their counterpart in dependent and servile followers. The vassals unconditionally promoted the personal interests, of whatever nature, of their caudillo, and the caudillo in turn protected his followers and bestowed such favors upon them as he was able to command and as their services warranted. Allegiances tended to be personal rather than political or ideological; honor was measured in terms of fealty to the person of one's caudillo and of paternal concern for one's vassals and serfs. The Mexican peasant, therefore, as well as the Mexican in general, tied his personal welfare to the destinies of a caudillo. Once an individual had entered the train of a given caudillo, he generally was reluctant to change his allegiance as long as his caudillo was satisfactorily furthering his personal interests.

Mexico's low degree of economic integration as well as its relatively poor communications contributed to the formation of strong regionalist sentiments among the Mexican people. Individuals of one region felt a certain lack of identification with those from other regions; consequently, when the armed conflict began, the peasants tended to follow leaders from their native regions. This strong regionalist sentiment facilitated the setting of peasant against peasant. (Further on we will examine attempts to divide the peasantry.) The Yaqui warrior from Sonora within the Constitutionalist army, for example, fought against the *zapatistas* virtually as if they were foreigners.

This lack of class consciousness on the part of many peasants was augmented by the ignorance, poverty and generally benighted circumstances in which they lived. That is to say, many peasants participated in the conflict in order to find escape from the straitened circumstances of their lives in the expansive life of loot and adventure which many revolutionary armies offered. The motives of these individuals were personalist; it little mattered to them that they might have to fight against the legitimate demands of their brothers.

Regionalism and opportunism tended to reinforce the influence of *caudillismo* among the peasants. The peasantry divided its allegiance among a number of local caudillos who in turn generally owed allegiance to a more powerful caudillo, such as Villa, Zapata or Carranza. All these caudillos offered to promote the peasants' interests in one way or another, and all spoke of satisfying the peasants' basic demand for land. Hence, considering the nature of the caudillo-vassal relationship, it was difficult for any one of these caudillos to unite the entire peasantry behind him.

Zapata's movement acquire distinction and historical prestige to the degree that it overcame localist, personalist and opportunist motivations and struggled undeviatingly and intransigently for social goals. Although Zapata's peasant followers undoubtedly saw him as a caudillo who could defend their interests, Zapata nevertheless gave a social character to his movement by orienting the struggles of his followers toward the realization of a broad program of social and political reforms. In respect to its social rather than personalist orientation, Zapata's movement was similar to the other great social reform movements in Mexico's history. José María Morelos struggled intransigently for the independence of Mexico from Spain; Benito Juárez for the supremacy of the civil state over the Church and military, and Zapata for the destruction of Mexico's semi-feudal order through land reform. The Constitutionalists, however, were able to take advantage of the influences of *caudillismo,* regionalism and opportunism in Mexican life to thwart Zapata's efforts to unify the entire peasantry under his leadership.

Where the *zapatistas* failed to attract ample support from broad sectors of the Mexican population, the *carrancistas* succeeded. That is to say, the Constitutionalists were able to form a national front composed of elements of the peasantry, the proletariat, the urban petty-bourgeoisie and the bourgeoisie. They were able, especially, to attract greater support than other revolutionary factions from the intellectuals and other members of the urban petty-bourgeoisie and bourgeoisie. The Constitutionalists' success at attracting support from broad sectors of the population undoubtedly contributed to their victory over the *zapatistas*. They owed their victory, in addition, to the facility with which they acquired arms and munitions abroad, especially in the United States. The Constitutionalists' military might, in turn, increased their following among those elements of the population who from opportunistic motives wished to be on the winning side, whichever it might be.

Carranza drew support from the more radical elements of the nascent bourgeoisie, the petty-bourgeoisie and the urban proletariat by making general promises for social reform. For example, in a speech delivered in Sonora on September 24, 1913, Carranza expressed interest in establishing a political democracy in Mexico, in achieving greater freedom and equality of opportunity for Mexicans, in distributing the wealth more equitably, in dividing lands, in providing laws in benefit of workers and peasants, and in achieving independence from the influences of foreign imperialist nations. He did not go into details on these matters.[17] (It will be recalled that, in contrast, Zapata's Plan of Ayala, issued in 1911, contained detailed proposals for land reform and upheld the political reforms proposed in Madero's Plan of San Luís.)

On July 9, 1914, Carranza presented a statement of his revolutionary position to Dr. Henry Allen Tupper, Special Peace Commissioner of the International Peace Forum, in which he declared that the Constitutionalist movement embodied a true social revolution. However, he did not indicate any details of the social reforms which the Constitutionalists proposed to carry out.[18] In a speech delivered in Matamoros, Tamaulipas, on November 29, 1915, Carranza, continuing the vague and vacuous style which characterized his speeches, especially when they touched upon questions of social reform, repeated almost verbatim the concepts he had expressed in Sonora in 1913. He referred to land reform in the same terms he used two years previously, stating that the revolution was "not only the division of lands," without going into further details.[19]

Carranza's promises of labor reforms drew him support from elements of the urban proletariat. These workers were attracted especially by the more radical elements within the Constitutionalist movement who presented themselves as *obreristas* (pro-labor) as well as *agraristas* (pro-peasant). Although the *zapatistas* also offered the workers reforms and sought their support, the workers, for the reasons suggested above, were attracted more by the currents of urban-oriented liberalism within the Constitutionalist movement than by the agrarian-oriented, petty-bourgeois radicalism of the *zapatistas*. Also, by the time the *Casa del Obrero Mundial* made a formal pact of alliance with the Constitutionalists in February 1915, the *villistas* and *zapatistas* had proved themselves unable to dominate Mexico. The *carrancistas*, in short, offered more probabilities of victory.[20]

The *carrancistas* encouraged the disunity which existed within the Mexican peasantry due to the influences of *caudillismo*, regionalism and opportunism by promising land and other reforms to the peasantry while giving the *carrancista* soldiers, who were largely of peasant origin, license to sack and pillage, especially in their campaigns against the *zapatistas*. The Constitutionalists' success in attracting the support of a portion of the peasantry and in preventing the peasants from unifying around a radical program such as the *zapatistas* offered was perhaps the factor which most contributed to their victory in the revolution. The lack of unity among the peasants enabled the Constitutionalists to defeat the *villistas* and to contain the revolutionaries of the South and thus to behead the movement by the assassination of Zapata.

The *carrancistas* offered land reform in a decree of December 12, 1914, and in a law of January 6, 1915.[21] As we have seen, the latter provided for the restitution of lands which had been illegally alienated from village communities and for the granting of lands to villages which were unable to acquire sufficient land for their needs by the process of restitution. The law restricted the lands subject to expropriation to those immediately adjacent to the petitioning communities and placed the authority for implementing the reform in first instance in the hands of the state governors. It is noteworthy that the *carrancistas* proclaimed these measures of land reform during the darkest days of their conflict with the *villistas* and *zapatistas* and before they had won any significant military victory over their opponents. It seems rather obvious that the purpose of these measures was to divide the allegiance of the peasants.[22] The law of January 6, 1915, which was drafted by Luís Cabrera, was Carranza's answer to Zapata's Plan of Ayala. But while Zapata was sincere in his proposals for thoroughgoing land reform, Carranza showed that he was not when he did little to implement these measures once he became president.

Finally, Carranza adamantly opposed military or political intervention by foreign, chiefly United States, imperialism in Mexico's domestic affairs. He passed legislation, which included the imposition of relatively high taxes, to control the foreign-owned oil industry. American oil interests reacted by pressuring for intervention by U.S. armed forces, but Woodrow Wilson opposed their efforts. Also, Carranza's regime recovered for the Mexican nation a great deal of the national lands which had been alienated to private persons, many of them foreigners, during the Díaz regime. Carranza's defense of Mexico's right to determine its own destiny appealed to some of the deepest sentiments of the Mexican people.[23]

Constitutionalist military commanders and governors initiated moderate reforms in some regions of the Republic during the course of the armed revolution, thereby whetting the appetite of the workers and peasants. These reforms provided, in some states, for shorter working hours, minimum wages, Sunday rest, abolition of debt peonage and suppression of estate or "company" stores (*tiendas de raya*) on the haciendas. The partitioning of lands among the peasants was initiated in some regions.[24]

The more radical elements within the Constitutionalist movement struggled for the realization of more drastic reforms. These elements, which included individuals such as Francisco J. Mújica, Heriberto Jara, Esteban B. Calderón, Rafael Martínez de Escobar and Luís G. Monzón, formed a radical or "Jacobin" group in the constituent congress which drafted the Constitution of 1917. Obregón lent support to this faction. The radicals objected to the almost purely political character of the project of reforms to the Constitution of 1857 which Carranza had presented to the congress for approval. As a consequence of the radicals' pressure, article 27 of Carranza's project, which dealt with property rights and eminent domain, was given the progressive content which distinguishes it, and an entirely new article, 123, was drafted as a charter of rights for the working class. In addition, the radicals played a role in giving articles 3 and 130, which dealt with church-state relationships and the role of the church in education, an even greater anti-clerical content than they had possessed in the Constitution of 1857.[25] According to one author, Carranza accepted these radical additions to his projected constitution because he was afraid that General Obregón might lead a coup against him if he did not.[26] Indeed, Carranza's acceptance of these additions appears somewhat hypocritical since he did little to give them practical effect during his presidency.[27]

In addition to gaining the allegiance of some of the more radical elements of the population, Carranza attracted support from the more conservative sectors of the bourgeoisie and the petty-bourgeoisie, as well as from survivors of the old order. Several factors contributed to Carranza's success in this respect.

Carranza was the more conservative of the principal revolutionary leaders and thereby inspired greater confidence in many property owners. Carranza himself was a well-to-do member of the rural bourgeoisie and had served as a federal senator and as governor of Coahuila in the epoch of Porfirio Díaz. He also was better prepared than Zapata or Villa in the technicalities of politics, diplomacy and legal and financial matters, although it must be noted that his abilities were not outstanding. Furthermore, the distinguishing characteristic of most of his closest associates was their subservience to their chief and their ability to get rich quick.[28]

The military strength of the Constitutionalists also attracted the moderates. That is to say, after the Conventionists proved themselves unable to dominate Mexico militarily at the end of 1914 and early in 1915, many property owners, including foreign investors, turned to the Constitutionalists as the only force capable of bringing peace and stability to the country. Also, once the Huerta regime was destroyed, the Constitutionalists, the more conservative of the principal revolutionary factions, represented the lesser evil for the survivors of the old order, although many of these individuals could not accept Carranza in any form because he had led the Constitutionalist movement against Huerta's attempt to restore the sacred *ancien régime*.

Although Carranza expressed a general interest in social reforms on several occasions during the revolution, he never elaborated a detailed program of thoroughgoing reforms. Those reforms which he did propose in his Veracruz decrees were limited in character and, more important, they were implemented with considerable restraint. This vagueness and, especially, this restraint in practice apparently appealed to the more moderate sectors of the Mexican population. In practice, little land was distributed among the peasants and a ferocious war of blood and terror was unleashed upon the radical peasant followers of Zapata; strikes were broken and militant workers jailed; and considerable restraint was exercized in the government's efforts to enforce the anti-imperialist provisions of the Constitution of 1917.

In brief, the Constitutionalists offered something to everyone. On the one hand, they offered land reform to the peasants, labor reform to the workers, pillage, prestige and promotions to the members of the army, stimulation of small and medium business enterprise to the petty-bourgeoisie and nascent bourgeoisie, and opposition to foreign imperialism to all these classes. On the other hand, they promised restraint in all these matters to the more conservative elements of society, such as the large land-owners, the big capitalists and the foreign investors. The tactic of organizing their movement around a political plan which called merely for the restoration of constitutional order in Mexico after the Huerta coup contributed to the Constitutionalist's success in attracting a panorama of elements to their movement. Anyone who had an anti-feudal, democratic or anti-imperialist spirit, no matter how mild, could take up such a banner. Those of more radical inclination who joined the Constitutionalist movement could content themselves with general promises for reform and with the few concrete measures which were taken. The radical banner of the *zapatistas,* on the other hand, would attract only the more extreme segments of the population. In their compro-mising, "something for everybody" spirit, the Constitutionalists resembled the official political parties formed later, the *Partido Nacional Revolucionario* (PNR), the *Partido de la Revolución Mexicana* (PRM), and the *Partido Revolucionario Institucional* (PRI).

Due to the conflicting interests contained within it, such an alliance as the Constitutionalists had formed was always some-what unstable and threatened to break apart if one of the groups composing it went too far in restricting the interests of the other component groups. Once in control of the nation, Carranza com-mitted the error of giving too much support to the rightist ele-ments of the coalition. In so doing, Carranza was not really changing character. He had been politically moderate all along and had never promised to implement a genuinely radical pro-gram of social reforms. He had, however, permitted radical ele-ments within his movement to nurse such hopes, presumably be-cause the support of these elements was essential to him to attain victory. These elements were powerful and could not be expected to wait forever for the regime in power to begin to implement some of the reforms, such as the distribution of lands, for which they had fought. In the Aguascalientes Convention, these more radical elements had voted to accept the Plan of Ayala in prin-ciple and also to accept Carranza's resignation of the executive power of the nation. The radicals had done an about face when Carranza had refused to resign his authority and had thereby made an armed conflict inevitable between his forces and those of his strongest military rival, Francisco Villa. In so doing, these *carrancista* chieftains apparently followed the dictates of their personal interests. They had tied their fortunes to Carranza's star; their future depended upon the fate of their caudillo. Furthermore, it would have been difficult for many of them to work with Villa; they could never have felt safe in his hands. Hence, they stuck with their master.

The distribution of lands among the peasants scarcely moved during Carranza's term as constitutional president (1917-1920) and it was his more progressive followers who were responsible for much of such distribution as did occur. By the end of 1919, the Carranza regime had distributed the pittance of 173,000 hectares among 51,400 beneficiaries.[29] In the summer of 1916, Carranza had closed the *Casa del Obrero Mundial* and he had also issued a decree which provided the death penalty for workers who struck or conspired to strike in public service industries, who damaged their employer's property during a strike, who caused public disturbances, or who prevented strike-breakers from entering struck establishments. Soldiers were used to break strikes and strikers were carried before military tribunals.[30]

Carranza continued his anti-labor policies during his term as Constitutional president and although labor was able to make organizational gains, forming the *Confederación Regional de Obreros Mexicanos* (CROM) in 1918, the government maintained control of the labor movement. Rosendo Salazar, former member of the *Casa del Obrero Mundial*, has indicated the true measure of Carranza's attitude toward labor. According to Salazar, when a delegation (of which he was a member) from the *Casa* met with Carranza after the Constitutionalists had occupied Mexico City in August 1914, "instead of finding a sympathizer of our *Casa*, we found a reserved man; he admonished us, saying, with complete frankness, that we should create mutualist societies because he did not find labor unionism to his liking."[31]

Finally, as previously observed, Carranza's regime exercized restraint in enforcing the anti-imperialist provisions of the Constitution of 1917, although it should be noted that America's armed power, which was always at least a potential threat to Mexico, undoubtedly played a role in this respect.

The continued drift to the right of Carranza's regime, as well as its inability to quell the revolutionaries of the South and restore peace to the countryside, created discontent and disaffection within the Constitutionalist ranks and especially among its more radical elements. Carranza took the final step toward alienating his followers when he named a civilian diplomat little associated with the revolution as his candidate for the presidency, thereby alienating the army as well as revolutionaries in general. Obregón, who had retired to his ranch in Sonora in 1917 after having led the Constitutionalist army to victory in the revolution, overthrew Carranza quite easily with a military coup in 1920. The new regime took measures to placate the workers, peasants and urban petty-bourgeoisie, including the distribution of land, especially in Morelos, and made peace with the remaining *zapatistas*.[32]

Obregón had formed an anti-feudal, anti-imperialist and bourgeois-democratic front similar in some respects to that which Zapata had sought to organize. However, in addition to appealing to Mexico's more radical elements, Obregón continued Carranza's policies of moderation and compromise with respect to the conservative elements of society, such as the large landowners. The Obregón regime thereby achieved a greater national and international consensus than Carranza's or Zapata's movement had been able to attain by adopting a position intermediate between the moderate tendencies of the former and the radical stance of the latter. This national unity was achieved though only after Zapata's movement had been virtually destroyed by blood and terror in the preceeding years. The more radical elements now had to work for their goals within the framework of a capitalistically structured social order in which the former Constitutionalist army was the ultimate arbiter of social conflicts.

Our analysis thus leads us to the conclusion that a complex and contradictory process appears to have been at work during the revolution which resulted in the reestablishment of national unity and relative social peace in the Obregón regime. During the struggle between the revolutionaries and the Huerta regime, the principal conflict had been between elements of the bourgeoisie, the petty-bourgeoisie, the working class and the peasantry on the one hand, and the *hacendados,* the Díaz bureaucracy and army, and some bourgeois elements, on the other. The revolutionary movement contained conflicting interests within it, however, and upon the overthrow of the Huerta regime, various of the components of that movement began to fight among themselves. The causes of this struggle were profound. The more moderate elements of the bourgeoisie and the petty-bourgeoisie who dominated the Constitutionalist movement threatened to leave a part of the old order intact; especially, they apparently intended to leave a great part of the land in the hands of the large landowners. The more radical sector of the peasantry and elements of the radical urban petty-bourgeoisie could not accept such an outcome to the revolution. In opposing the Constitutionalists, these more radical elements were merely continuing a struggle for land reform which they had carried on against the Díaz, Madero and Huerta regimes in the past.

This conflict between the Constitutionalists and the Conventionists, in turn, tended to sharpen the contradiction latent within the Constitutionalist movement between the more radical elements of the nascent bourgeoisie, the urban petty-bourgeoisie, the workers and the peasants, on the one hand, and the more conservative elements of the bourgeoisie and the urban petty-bourgeoisie on the other. The survivors of the old order, such as large landowners, tended to reinforce the conservative faction within the Constitutionalist movement.

The Obregón coup in 1920 changed the relationship of forces within the Constitutionalist movement. The more conservative members of that movement lost their control of political power and the moderate and radical elements moved to the fore. Obregón occupied a position more or less mid-way between the radical and conservative factions of his party. The greater influence of the radicals within the regime made it possible for Obregón to come to terms with the revolutionaries of the South, that is to say, with the more radical sector of the peasantry and the elements of the radical urban petty-bourgeoisie associated with it. Equally important in this *détente* with the *zapatistas*, however, was the fact that the revolution of the South was exhausted from years of conflict against overwhelming odds. The more radical segments of Mexican society had no choice for the time being but to submit to the new bourgeois order.

Obregón's coup brought the armed phase of the revolution to an end, it gave greater influence within the government to the more radical bourgeois and petty-bourgeois elements among the Constitutionalists, and it placed Mexico's modern program of agrarian, labor and educational reforms upon a firm foundation. It also cemented the bases of a political power structure which, with modifications, exists to this day in Mexico. Nevertheless, the reforms which that regime and the subsequent regime of Plutarco Elías Calles initiated were not thoroughgoing enough to destroy Mexico's old social order; most of the nation's large landed estates remained intact. The distinction of dealing a body blow of structural changes from which the old order could not recover belongs to the regime of Lázaro Cárdenas (1934-1940).

The United States intervened in various ways during the Mexican Revolution in order to protect the interests of American investors in Mexico. In opposing the anti-imperialist tendencies of the revolution, the United States tended also to thwart the *complete* realization of the anti-feudal and bourgeois-democratic goals of the revolution. That is to say, those elements of Mexican society which were more likely to take direct action against American investments in Mexico were also those which were most resolutely anti-feudal and pro-democratic. In opposing anti-imperialist measures, therefore, the United States encouraged the moderates among the revolutionary forces who, although they might oppose direct intervention by the United States in

Mexico, did not contemplate taking drastic measures against the interests of American investors. At the same time, these moderates proposed to implement only rather limited reforms in Mexico's economic and political structure. Thus, although the U.S. government had serious conflicts with the Constitutionalists over the occupation of Veracruz in 1914 (and later over the invasion of northern Mexico by American troops in 1916-1917) and for a time in 1915 apparently considered supporting Villa instead of Carranza, the influence of the United States, if only over the long run and at times indirectly, served to bolster the moderates within the Constitutionalist movement. The United States granted diplomatic recognition to the Carranza regime in October 1915.

The U.S. government continued to apply its neo-colonial policies with success during the Obregón regime. The relatively limited character of Obregón's reforms in Mexico may be explained in part as arising from his personal moderation in this respect. As a representative of the nascent rural bourgeoisie, Obregón never set himself the task of implementing a thoroughgoing distribution of lands similar to that envisioned in the Plan of Ayala. It can also be explained in part as a consequence of Obregón's politics of compromise and accomodation, within the framework of capitalist property relationships, between conflicting social groups in Mexico. U.S. imperialism, however, also played an important role in determining Obregón's policies.

The United States withheld diplomatic recognition from the Obregón government in an effort to force that regime to formally recognize the non-retroactivity of Article 27 (described in next chapter) of the Constitution of 1917 in a treaty between the two nations. Obregón, as Carranza before him, expressed his willingness to abide by the non-retroactivity principle, but he refused to formalize it in a treaty. In 1923, however, with the threat of a counterrevolution looming before Obregón's regime as new presidential elections approached, American and Mexican representatives negotiated the Bucareli agreements (which were not embodied in a formal treaty) in which Mexico, in effect, accepted the non-retroactivity of Article 27 and also agreed to the formation of a commission to adjudicate claims which had arisen between the two nations since 1868. As a consequence of these agreements, the United States accorded diplomatic recognition to Obregón's government and American military aide was forthcoming when the expected counterrevolution broke out shortly thereafter.

During the Obregón and Calles regimes, the influence of the U.S. neo-colonial policies served to thwart efforts to implement anti-imperialist measures, to weaken the influence of the more radical elements within these regimes, and to strengthen the moderates. These latter, a small group of military officers, capitalists and landowners grown wealthy as a consequence of the revolution dominated the Mexican nation under Calles's aegis. The Cárdenas regime represented a return to the forefront, principally as a consequence of renewed revolutionary agitation of Mexico's workers and peasants, of the more radical and more nationalist bourgeois and petty-bourgeois elements within the revolutionary movement. The Cárdenas regime definitively broke the nation's semi-feudal land system and implemented important measures of nationalization of foreign enterprises.

CHAPTER VI

The Fate of *Zapatista* Ideology

I want to die a slave to principles, not to men.
— Emiliano Zapata

The men of the South did not win the armed conflict, but they did strongly influence the outcome of the revolution. Their struggle had at least played a part in forcing Constitutionalists to proclaim measures of agrarian reform in Vera Cruz in 1914-1915, and their victory over Pablo González's army in 1916 also lent strength to the radicals in the Constitutional Convention of 1916-1917. It was these radicals who succeeded in having the Carranza-led moderates acquiesce in the incorporation of advanced concepts of agrarian and labor reform into the Constitution of 1917.

Article 27 of the Constitution of 1917 provided for the restitution of lands which had been illegally alienated from village communities and for the granting of additional lands to those communities which could not attain sufficient lands for their needs under the first provision. In contrast, in addition to providing for the distribution of land by the processes of restitution and of expropriation by reason of public utility, the *zapatista* measures, which considerably antedated those of the Constitutionalists, provided for the nationalization of the properties of enemies of the revolution. Furthermore, in contrast to Article 27 of the Constitution, the *zapatistas* did not limit the lands subject to expropriation to those near the communities to receive lands, nor did they place the implementation of the agrarian reform in first instance in the hands of the state governors. Instead, the *zapatistas* left the initiative for land distribution with the people (at least in so far as the restitution of lands to villages was concerned); the state was merely to confirm the popular initiative and settle disputes. Also, the men of the South envisioned the extension of producers' and consumers' cooperatives in the countryside, as well as the creation of an effective system of rural credit.

On the other hand, Article 27 contained several advanced concepts which were not stated explicitly in the *zapatista* documents. It declared the Mexican nation to be the original owner of all lands and waters within the territorial limits and made the national ownership of subsoil deposits and waters inalienable, although concessions for their development could be given to private persons. In addition, this article stipulated that property rights could be modified in accordance with the public interest. These provisions served in subsequent decades as the legal basis for nationalizations of foreign properties and, in general, for state intervention in the economy. The Mexican state has come to play a central role in the nation's economic development. As indicated previously, the *zapatistas* proposed measures to control the exploitation of the subsoil, to restrict the operations of foreign enterprises in Mexico, and to modify property rights in accordance with the public interest. The spirit of these measures was similar to that of Article 27.

In practice, Obregón's regime and succeeding governments did not implement the agrarian reform with the swiftness and thoroughness that the *zapatista* program of reform envisioned. Nevertheless, the need for land reform had become a part of the national consciousness; succeeding "revolutionary" governments pursued the distribution of lands with greater or lesser intensity and sincerity. The agrarian reform made particular strides during the regime of Lázaro Cárdenas when the radical petty-bourgeoisie and elements of the nascent national bourgeoisie, with the active support and cooperation of the organized working class and the peasantry, implemented many reforms of anti-feudal, anti-imperialist and bourgeois-democratic spirit.

The agrarian reform, nevertheless, has never been completed. The peasants still clamor for land and, much to the detriment of Mexico's efforts to industrialize its economy, extremely low levels of living continue to prevail among the greater part of the more than one-half of the nation's population which lives in the countryside. Furthermore, the advances of modern science and technology have been applied only partially to Mexican agriculture. Mexico's agrarian problems may be the rock on which its revolution, in its present bourgeois form, will flounder.

Article 123 of the Constitution of 1917 included many of the labor reforms which Zapata's movement had called for in its program of political and social reforms as well as in other documents. Among other things, Article 123 provided for the right to organize unions and the right to strike, minimum wages, an eight-hour workday, abolition of child labor and of debt peonage, and safe and hygienic conditions of labor.

This article, however, also included a provision for compulsory arbitration of labor-capital disputes and introduced the concept of "licit" and "illicit" strikes. It contained the absurd and reactionary stipulation that "strikes will be licit when they have as their objective the achievement of equilibrium between the various factors of production, harmonizing the rights of capital and labor." As the *zapatistas* warned, these provisions implied grave threats to the rights of the workers and opened the door to government domination of the labor movement. Although the labor movement managed to achieve considerable unity and independence in the 1930's, these gains have since been undermined. The government has replaced many honest and independent labor leaders with flunkies whose principal concern is to get rich quick, even if they have to sell out the workers whom they supposedly represent. The system of compulsory arbitration permits the government to decide on the legality of strikes; the government has employed its police forces and even, on occasions, the army to impose its will when the workers have challenged its decisions. The achievement of a united and independent labor movement remains one of the principal goals of Mexico's progressive forces.

Article 115 of the Constitution provides for municipal freedom. The regimes in power, however, have not put this reform into practice. The *zapatista* ideal of municipal democracy, which they made real in the regions which they controlled during the revolution, has remained a goal of the progressive forces in Mexico.

Zapata's efforts to promote popular education, especially in the rural areas, were continued on a larger scale by the "revolutionary" governments, especially those of Álvaro Obregón, Plutarco Elías Calles and Lázaro Cárdenas. Thousands of schools were constructed in the countryside and the rural schoolteacher became the enlightener and protector of the rural poor. However, insufficient funds, harassment by local bosses, and opposition by the conservative forces sapped the initial revolutionary spirit of this program. Expenditures for education form the greatest single item in Mexico's national budget, but there is still a serious shortage of rural schools, and rural schoolteachers, in general, have lost their sense of professional dedication.

The Constitution of 1917 provided for a democratic political regime in Mexico, although at the same time it extended the powers of the central government and strengthened the power of the executive branch. These latter provisions have facilitated the president's autocratic control of the nation's political life but they have also increased the authority and flexibility of the state in managing the economic development of the nation. The *zapatistas* wished to establish a parliamentary democracy in Mexico and make all important laws subject to popular referendum. The revolutionaries of the South even went so far as to guarantee the people's right to revolution.

Mexico has made gains in democratizing its political life, but much remains to be achieved. Elections are still controlled by the government and *caudillismo* still prevails in Mexico's economic, social and political life. But the *zapatistas'* desire for economic liberty — for freedom from exploitation of man by man — and for popular control of the nation's political life remain the ideals of the Mexican people.

The Constitution of 1917 and the *zapatista* documents proposed to restrict the influence of foreign imperialism in Mexico, although they did not propose to eliminate foreign investments entirely. The Mexican nation has made considerable progress in recovering its national wealth and in affirming its independence from foreign interventionism. Foreign capitalist investors, however, still have powerful interests in the Mexican economy and foreign capitalist nations, principally the United States, still attempt to pressure the Mexican government to adopt policies favorable to imperialism. The Mexican nation has yet to decide "to be or not to be" in regard to foreign imperialism. Nevertheless, anti-imperialist sentiment is deeply rooted in the consciousness of the Mexican people; a frankly pro-imperialist regime could not survive for long in Mexico.

In summary, the reforms for which the *zapatistas* fought would have laid the bases for the democratization of the nation's political life; the recovery of national wealth in the hands of foreign capitalists and, consequently, increased independence from foreign meddling in Mexico's domestic affairs; more equitable distribution of wealth; greater equality of opportunity; improvement in popular education; and the achievement of higher levels of living. These goals have been at least partially achieved in practice. More important, Zapata's movement contributed to orienting the modern Mexican consciousness toward the attainment of these ends. The long and fierce struggle of Zapata and his followers finds its justification in the fact that, in the decades which have followed the armed conflict, the regimes in power have been confronted with great popular discontent whenever they have flagged in the pursuit of these ends.

These goals which Zapata's movement sought — economic development, more equitable distribution of wealth, higher levels of living, equality of opportunity, and individual and social self-determination — are the goals which the progressive forces of humanity have been seeking for centuries. In Zapata's day, when the productive forces of society were less developed than now, the realization of a democracy of small owners on the basis of a wide distribution of property among the nation's citizens could serve as the bases for at least the partial realization of these objectives. Even at that time, though, the development of productive forces had made such a wide distribution of property at least in part impracticable; consequently, the men of the South had to modify this traditional liberal solution to the problem of human freedom. The essence of the response of the *zapatistas* to modern capitalism and imperialism was to propose measures and to seek guarantees on the part of the state to promote and to defend the interests of the workers (the propertyless) and the small owners within the framework of capitalist—and imperialist—social relationships. The development of capitalism and imperialism soon demonstrated the inadequacy of such measures as means to achieve the transcendental goal of human material, social and spiritual freedom.

The progressive forces in contemporary Mexico seek to organize a national, anti-imperialist front which, under the guidance of the working class, will take control of the state power and construct a socialist regime in Mexico. This regime will guarantee the nation's independence from foreign imperialism, redistribute the income more equitably, promote economic development, raise levels of living, and foment democratic practices in all aspects of national life. Today socialism has replaced all forms of bourgeois liberalism as the road to human fulfillment.

The goals sought by the *zapatistas* may be summarized in one term: human freedom. Freedom through control by man over his material and social environment, so as to permit man to develop his distinctively human potentialities to the fullest. Although this end may never be attained in full, the Mexican people—as well as the rest of humanity—can continue to approach it. Social regimes which thwart human development cannot stand for long.

The words of Emiliano Zapata to Huerta in 1913 still have vitality for many Mexicans. "The Revolution has not triumphed. ... In your hands still is the will and the power to save it; but if, unfortunately, you do not, the shades of Cuauhtemoc, Hidalgo and Juárez and the heroes of all times will stir in their tombs to ask: What have you done with the blood of your brothers?"

The Literature On The
Zapatista-Carrancista Conflict

Various interpretations have been given of the causes for the conflict between the *zapatistas* and the *carrancistas*. During the course of the revolution, *carrancista* authors and lecturers either ignored the problem of explaining the reasons for their war with the men of the South or justified the conflict with allegations that the southerners were bandits or reactionaries. The Constitutionalists reflected their attitudes, for example, in a compilation of articles and speeches published in 1916, which included contributions by such prominent *carrancistas* as Álvaro Obregón, general-in-chief of the Constitutionalist forces and Secretary of War until May 1917; Isidro Fabela, Secretary of Foreign Affairs in Carranza's cabinet in 1913-1914; Felix Palavicini, Secretary of Public Instruction and Fine Arts in Carranza's cabinet in 1914-1916; Edmundo González-Blanco, Spanish writer and litterateur; José N. Macías, federal deputy during the governments of Porfirio Díaz and Francisco Madero and rector of the National University during Carranza's government; and Alfredo Breceda, Constitutionalist general and former private secretary of Carranza; several speeches by Carranza were included at the end of the book.

Although the theme of the work was Carranza and his movement, the contributors, in general, ignored the question of justifying Carranza's war upon the *zapatistas*. However, Macías, who, in addition to his other accomplishments mentioned above, drafted the project of reforms to the Constitution of 1857 which Carranza presented to the Constituent Convention of 1916-17, dealt with the problem and set the tone of *carrancista* thought when he said:

"As to the rest, Huerta, Zapata and Villa are brothers: the three of them are equally representatives of the lowest social depths because they sum up marveously all ignoble passions, all savage instincts, and all brutal lusts.

"Huerta, Villa and Zapata were engendered by ignorance and vice in a night of orgy and because of this, like Gargantua, their first word was *alcohol* and more *alcohol*.* Nourished on infected entrails and reared in mire, they have a special liking for pestilent nourishment. Educated among pariahs and thieves, they can live only by cursing and appropriating for themselves whatever they find in their paths. Totally lacking in morals and human respect, they sow death everywhere: human blood has an odor which allures their jackel sense of smell. For this reason, Huerta, Villa, and Zapata have always had their cortege of drunkards, thieves and assassins" (Palavicini, 48-9).

Neither Macías nor any other of the contributors to this work mentioned the problem of land reform in relation to the struggle between the Constitutionalists and the men of the South.

González-Blanco, Spanish writer associated with the Constitutionalists, in his work, *De Porfirio Díaz a Carranza* (1916), rejected the *zapatista* banner of land reform as fraudulent and denounced Zapata and his followers as bandits in the service of reaction. Thus, he declared: "Zapata, rebelling against Madero in order to continue his life of vandalism and barbarism and later against Carranza, has fallen into the hands of the *científicos* and sacristans and represents that ambiguous type who, since the Aguascalientes Convention, dilutes the revolutionary pill in the muddy waters of the reaction" (243). González-Blanco did not mention the intransigent demands of the *zapatistas* before Carranza for land reform, nor did he call attention to the distribution of lands undertaken by the *zapatistas* in the areas under their control.

Obregón, in his work, *Ocho Mil Kilómetros en Campaña* (1917), made no effort to explain the cause of the conflict be-

*Villa was a teetotaler.

tween the *carrancistas* and the men of the South and, indeed, made little reference at all to the *zapatistas*.

Writing in 1935, Luís Cabrera, one of the "unofficial" representatives of Carranza at the Cuernavaca parleys and Secretary of Finance in Carranza's cabinet in 1915-1917 and again in 1919-1920, stated that Zapata ceased to be a revolutionary when he broke with Madero. Cabrera thereby seemingly supported the *carrancista* allegation that the *zapatistas* were "reactionaries." (Urrea, pseud. for Luis Cabrera, 227.)*

Since the days of the revolutionary struggle, Zapata has become a national hero along with Carranza. Authors of works in general favorable to Carranza frequently praise Zapata as well, without attempting to resolve the apparent contradiction of this attitude. See, for example, the work of Alfonso Taracena, *Venustiano Carranza* (1963), which, although laudatory of Carranza, apparently accepts the *zapatista* account of the causes of their conflict with the *carrancistas* (242-43). Taracena thereby remains faithful to the interpretation of this conflict which he gave in *La Tragedia Zapatista* (1931).

There are still writers, however, who ignore the question of Carranza's relationship with Zapata. Thus, Francisco L. Urquizo, former Secretary of War and Navy under Carranza, made only one reference to Zapata, and that quite trivial, (p. 28) in his work, *Don Venustiano Carranza; El Hombre, el Politico, el Caudillo* (1939). In a revised and enlarged edition, *Carranza*; *El Hombre, el Político, el Caudillo, el Patriota* (1957), Urquizo still felt it unnecessary to mention the conflict between the Constitutionalists and the men of the South.

José Vasconcelos, lawyer, writer and Minister of Public Education in 1921-1924, in his *Breve Historia de México*

---

*One must be cautious, however, to infer that Cabrera thought in the same manner in 1914. In the 1930s Cabrera served as lawyer for the *Asociación Defensora de la Industria Henequenera* (Henequen Industry Defense Association), one of the most reactionary associations of large landowners and capitalists in Mexico at that time and, furthermore, he flirted with fascist "solutions" to Mexico's problems (352).

(1956) leaves rather unclear the motives for the conflict between
Zapata and Carranza except for his comment: "General Zapata,
on his part, did not recognize any authority in Carranza whom,
instigated by the demogogues and pettifoggers who surrounded
him, he rated as bourgeois and reactionary" (452).

Juan Barragán Rodríguez, Carranza's former chief of staff,
presents the contemporary *carrancista* interpretation of the
reasons for their conflict with the *zapatistas* in his work, *Historia
del Ejército y de la Revolución Constitucionalista*, (1946).
Barragan (II, 12, 28-29) claims that the Constitutionalists and
the southern revolutionaries could not come to an agreement
primarily because the latter insisted that Carranza accept the
Plan of Ayala unconditionally, and Article III of that plan
recognized Zapata as the Chief of the Revolution. In other words,
according to Barragán, the principal aim of the *zapatistas* was
to impose Zapata as the commander in chief of all the revolutionary armies and, possibly, as chief executive, pushing Carranza aside. Although this interpretation was also expressed
during the revolution, it was only until sometime after the armed
conflict ended that it became fashionable among certain writers.

Felix F. Palavicini, *Grandes de México* (1948), repeats this
theme (43) and Robert Quirk, *The Mexican Revolution* (1960),
apparently gives it much credence (63-68). Jesús Silva Herzog,
Mexican historian and economist, in his *Breve Historia de la
Revolución Mexicana* (II, 118), accepts essentially this same
thesis, alleging that the revolutionaries of the South and the
Constitutionalists fell out over Zapata's insistence that Carranza
submit to his authority and accept the Plan of Ayala unconditionally. Silva Herzog, nevertheless, recognizes the social
orientation of Zapata's movement. Thus, when he attended the
Aguascalientes Convention in 1914, as a reporter, he wrote:
"It cannot be denied that it was after the arrival of the *zapatistas*
that revolutionary principles, economic reforms and govermental
programs began to be talked about. The *zapatistas* gave ideological content to the Convention." (II, 13.) Further on in the same

report, however, Silva Herzog expressed doubts concerning Zapata's motive in failing to give full authority to his delegation to the Convention (II, 132).*

The *zapatistas* have quite a different interpretation of the reasons for their conflict with the *carrancistas*. According to the men of the South, Carranza was a typical opportunistic *caudillo* whose primary concern was to impose himself as president of Mexico. As a social revolutionary, claim the *zapatistas,* Carranza was quite moderate; he had no intention of implementing a thoroughgoing land reform in Mexico. Zapata was intransigent with the Constitutionalists simply because he distrusted the motives of Carranza and his principal associates. Zapata insisted that Carranza accept the Plan of Ayala, continues the argument, only in order to ensure the realization of the agrarian provision of that Plan, which provided for the thoroughgoing distribution of land in Mexico, and the political provisions (expressed in Article XII), which provided that upon the victory of the revolution a junta of the principal revolutionary chiefs would elect an interim president who in turn would hold national elections. Zapata by no means sought to impose himself as Mexico's chief executive or as commander in chief of the constitutionalist army. (See the works cited previously by Magaña, Díaz Soto y Gama, Dromundo, the article by Octavio Paz in Meléndez, Rittenhouse, and Taracena. In addition, see Roberto Blanco Moheno, *Crónica de la Revolución Mexicana* (Mexico, 1957), I, 228-29, 237.

The *zapatista* interpretation seems the more realistic of the two. Considering the content of Article XII of the Plan of Ayala,

*The Convention invited the *zapatistas* to send a delegation shortly after it opened its sessions on October 10, 1914. Zapata accepted the invitation and immediately formed a commission of 26 members, but informed the Convention that all his principal chiefs must be represented (in accordance with the Plan of Ayala), which would take some time to arrange because of poor communications and the great distances at which some of his forces operated. Until his delegation was complete, it would have only a voice but no vote in the Convention (Díaz Soto y Gama, 182, 196).

Article III which named Zapata "Chief of the Revolution" did not in any way seek to usurp the executive authority of the nation for Zapata or to deprive Carranza of his position as "First Chief" of the Constitutionalist army. In the public documents of the *zapatistas*, Zapata frequently was referred to, or referred to himself as the "Chief of the Revolution in the Southern and Central States of the Republic" or as the "General-in-Chief of the Liberator Army." Zapata never assumed a title as ambitious as Carranza's "First Chief of the Constitutionalist Army in Charge of the Executive Power."

According to former *zapatista* Octavio Paz, Zapata was completely free from personal political ambitions and discouraged adulation of his person, claiming that idolators corrupted public men. Paz claimed that Zapata always made it clear that he did not aspire to public office and, on several occasions, even made formal commitments with his principal military leaders not to accept such offices. Municipal elections were held with absolute freedom in the areas which his forces controlled, in contrast to electoral practices in regions which the Constitutionalists dominated. Zapata, continued Paz, frequently declared that he did not aspire to the presidency and would not accept that office if offered him. He proposed to remain in arms until land reform was made a reality and then to retire to private life. There is nothing either in Zapata's actions or in his public or private statements which belies this exposition of his motives (see Meléndez, I, 323-24).

In public statements, letters and other documents, the *zapatistas* consistently showed concern for the acceptance and fulfullment by the revolution of the Plan of Ayala's provisions for agrarian reform and for the selection of an interim-president by the principal revolutionary chieftains of the republic. There is never any indication in these documents of a desire to impose Zapata as the "First Chief" or to charge him with the executive authority of the nation. In this writer's opinion, Zapata would have accepted Carranza as president – as he was willing to accept Madero – if the chief of the Constitutionalists had given genuine indications that he would implement a thoroughgoing land reform in Mexico and if a convention of revolutionary chieftains had freely designated him to fulfill the executive function.

Zapata expressed his attitude toward the imposition of political authorities upon the Mexican people to one of Huerta's peace emissaries in April 1913.

"As for the propositions which you make me, referring to that which suggests I designate the governor of this state, I would never usurp that faculty which corresponds, according to the ideals which we defend, to the junta of the principal revolutionaries of this entity, a junta in which I would take part, not in the role of dictator, but as a simple member to voice my vote. ... I, in my character as citizen and revolutionary leader, would never designate political authorities who should be designated by the representatives of a collectivity" (Magaña, III, 120).

Zapata made these concepts quite clear again in a manifesto which he issued in August 1914 shortly before he met with Carranza's representatives in Cuernavaca. Zapata claimed that as a consequence of their bitter experiences in the past the Mexican people now "with reason fear that the liberators of today are going to be the same as the *caudillos* of yesterday" and went on to explain that "for this reason the agrarian revolution, distrusting *caudillos* who accredit the triumph to themselves, has adopted as precaution and guarantee the most just precept that it be all the revolutionary chieftains of the nation who elect the First Magistrate and the Interim President who must convoke elections, because the agrarian revolution well knows that the revolution and, with it, the fate of the Republic depend upon the interim government" (Magaña, V, 20).

The document went on to state two conditions for establishing peace in Mexico.

"There is still time to reflect and to avoid conflict. If the chief of the Constitutionalists considers himself sufficiently popular to stand the test of subjecting himself to the vote of the revolutionaries, let him submit himself to it without vacilation. And if the Constitutionalists truly care for the people and know their exigencies, let them render homage to the sovereign will by accepting with sincerity and without reticence the three great principles consigned in the Plan of Ayala: expropriation of lands by reason of public utility, confiscation of the properties of the enemies of the people and restitution of lands which have been despoiled from individuals and communities" (Magaña, V, 20-21).

The manifesto did not mention any other conditions for coming to an understanding with the Constitutionalists; much less did it give the slightest indication of a desire to impose Zapata upon the Mexican people as chief executive or as the commander in chief of the Constitutionalist army.

In a letter to President Woodrow Wilson, dated August 23, 1914, Zapata lucidly explained the objectives of his movement and the significance of his insistence that the Plan of Ayala be fulfilled to the letter (Magaña, V, 108-12 and Reyes, 82-7). Zapata explained that the revolution had its origins in the monopolization of Mexico's lands by a few large landowners and that the principal objective of the revolutionaries was to break this monopoly and redistribute the lands. Zapata continued:

"One can affirm . . .that there will be no peace in Mexico until the Plan of Ayala is raised to the rank of law or constitutional precept and is fulfilled in all its parts.

"This is necessary not only in regards to the social question, that is, to the necessity of land distribution, but also in reference to the political question, that is to say, to the manner of designating the interim president who must convoke elections and begin to put the social reform into practice.

"The country is tired of impositions; it will no longer tolerate the imposition of masters or leaders; it wishes to take part in the designation of its political authorities, and since it is a question of an interim government which has to emanate from the revolution and give guarantees to the latter, it is logical and it is just that it be the genuine representatives of the revolution, that is to say, the chiefs of the armed movement, who effect the naming of the interim president. Thus disposes article twelve of the Plan of Ayala against the wishes of Don Venustiano Carranza and of his circle of ambitious politicians who pretend that Carranza scale to the presidency by surprise or, better said, by a stroke of audacity and imposition."

Indeed, it was Carranza, not Zapata, who was preeminently concerned with imposing himself upon Mexico as the commander in chief of the revolutionary armies and as the chief executive of the nation. Carranza's demand that the *zapatistas* join their forces with the Constitutionalists and accept Carranza's authority amounted to a demand for the complete surrender of the Liberator Army of the South. His desire to impose himself at all costs as chief executive of the Mexican nation is evidenced by his refusal to renounce his claim to the chief executiveship before the convention of revolutionary leaders held in Aguascalientes, even though the delegates, the majority of whom were *carrancistas*, voted to accept his resignation.

REFERENCE NOTES

(Full bibliographical data will be found in the List of Works Cited, under the name of the author.)

CHAPTER I

1. Magaña, I, 77. See also McBride, 142-44.
2. Simpson, 36.
3. The following account of Zapata's life and of the vicisitudes of the *zapatistas* in the revolutionary conflict is based upon material presented in the works of Magaña, I-V; Díaz Soto y Gama; Meléndez, I, 315-78; Dromundo; Rittenhouse; Valverde; and Taracena, *La Tragedia Zapatista*. This latter work is an amplification of material presented by the same author in his *En el Vértigo de la Revolución Mexicana*, which the author in turn amplified and published as the well known work, *Mi Vida en el Vértigo de la Revolución Mexicana*. Sotelo Inclán gives an excellent account of the struggle of Anenecuilco to defend its lands and its autonomy from pre-Cortesian times to the outbreak of the Revolution in 1910 and also provides (169-200) a valuable account of Zapata's formation as a revolutionary leader. Rosa E. King relates her experiences in Morelos during the revolution; Pinchon's book is a biography of Zapata in English. For an account of Zapata's amours and the fate of his descendants, see Gill.
4. Meléndez, I, 335-40; Cumberland, 172-84; Ross, 188-202; Magaña, I, 197-261; Taracena, *La Tragedia Zapatista*, 17-20.
5. Ross, 250-51; Cumberland, 182-84; Magaña, II, 63-79; Taracena, *La Tragedia Zapatista*, 20-4; Meléndez, I, 340-41.
6. Ross, 251; Cumberland, 183.
7. Ross, 202; Cumberland, 182-84.
8. Ross, 241; Díaz Soto y Gama, 122.
9. Ross, 242-46.
10. Díaz Soto y Gama, 121.
11. Silva Herzog, *Trayectoria Ideológica*, 37-9.
12. Fabela, I, 63.
13. King, 140.
14. Díaz Soto y Gama, 141.
15. Magaña, III, 116.
16. Quoted in Obregón, 251.
17. Breceda, II, 197-201.
18. Barragán Rodríguez, II, 44; 39-41.

19. Silva Herzog, *Breve Historia*, II, 124-25.
20. Barragán Rodríguez, I, 683.
21. Magaña, IV, 242-43; III, 280-82.
22. Taracena, *Venustiano Carranza*, 241-42.
23. Palavicini, II.
24. Breceda, I, 441.
25. *Documentos, Revolución y Régimen Constitucionalista*, I, 497-98.
26. Breceda, I, 435, 499.
27. Magaña, IV, 247-71; V, 12-14. Magaña presents the *zapatista* account of these interviews; I have not found a *carrancista* account.
28. *Ibid.*, IV, 247-71; V, 72-102; Díaz Soto y Gama, 173-81.
29. For a discussion and justification of the assumption of sovereignty by the Aguascalientes Convention, see Confidential Agency, esp. 1-22.
30. For a lucid eye-witness account of the entry of the *zapatistas* into the capital, see Ramírez Plancarte, 241-55.
31. Meléndez, I, 366-67.
32. For information on the Aguascalientes Convention, see Magaña, V, 118-360; Basave del Castillo Negrete, IV; Ramírez Plancarte, 73-307, 375-513, *passim*; Taracena, *La Tragedia Zapatista*, 51-2, 54, *passim*; and Quirk, 153-58, 165-79, 228-52, *passim*.
33. Several authors attribute Obregón's victory to the fact that the president of the Convention government, General Eulalio Gutiérrez, did not provide the defenders with adequate arms and ammunition. Taracena (*La Tragedia Zapatista*, 49) states that "the government of General Gutiérrez took elements [of war] away from the defending *zapatistas*." Valverde declares that "the *zapatista* generals realized that they could not undertake the defense of Puebla because the munitions which the President of the Convention sent were blanks" (159). See also Dromundo, 115.
34. Palavicini, 258.
35. Meléndez, I, 371.
36. Magaña, III, 257-59, 264, 267-70; Rittenhouse, 318-19; Díaz Soto y Gama, 226-27, 287; Meléndez, I, 323, 325-33, 350, 371, 372-75, *passim*; Chevalier, 169-72, 185. For comments on shortcomings in the organization and discipline of the *zapatista* forces, see Ramírez Plancarte, 401-06; Valverde, 158; and King, 222-23.
37. Meléndez, I, 373.
38. Dromundo, 160. For additional comments on the effectiveness of the *zapatistas'* guerrilla warfare, see King, 78, 88-9, 130-31.
39. *Méjico Revolucionario*, 127.

40. Taracena, *La Tragedia Zapatista*, 29, 36, 39, 70, 71, 74; Valverde, 179, 180, 185; Dromundo, 81, 82, 84, 88, 108, 117-18, 122-23, 146, 147, 159, 161-62, 171, 185; Díaz Soto y Gama, 110-13, 157, 226, 228, 233; Meléndez, I, 339-40, 347-48, 349, 350, 351, 354, 374; King, 89-94, 130-31, 298, 301-02; Reyes, 105.
41. Taracena, *La Tragedia Zapatista*, 74.
42. Magaña, I, 39-40.
43. Díaz Soto y Gama, 116-18, 274-79, 274-76. See also Chevalier, 171, and Meléndez, I, 351, 352.
44. Meléndez, I, 321.
45. Taracena, *La Tragedia Zapatista*, 12.
46. Magaña, III, 267, 269-70.
47. Reyes, 109.
48. *Ibid.*, 105.
49. Chevalier, 186.
50. For interpretations of Mexican-American relations during the Mexican Revolution, see Fabela, Link, Parkes, Quirk, and Cline.

CHAPTER II

1. For example, see Magaña, I, 228-29, *passim*.; Dromundo, 107-11, 201-05; Rittenhouse, 370-71; Gruening, 310-11; Tannenbaum, *The Mexican Agrarian Revolution*, 159-63.
2. For example, see Basave del Castillo Negrete, IV, 76-93; Magaña, II, 22-36, 58-62; Dunn; Quirk, 290-91, *passim*.
3. Magaña, I, 132-34.
4. Rittenhouse, 167-68.
5. Magaña, II, 83-7.
6. Rittenhouse, 232-33, 237.
7. Magaña, II, 65-7, 140; III, 252-57; IV, 203-06, 205; V, 17-21, 19, 102-03. Also Dromundo, 90-5.
8. This letter is reproduced in Magaña, IV, 308-10. *See also Chevalier*, 180.
9. Magaña, V, 118-360, 240-43, 232-39; and Basave del Castillo Negrete.
10. Magaña, IV, 247-75; V, 12-4, 75-102; Sala, 23-5, *passim*.
11. Rittenhouse, 305-17.
12. Dromundo, 165; the entire manifesto is reproduced, 162-66.
13. *Ibid.*, 154.
14. Magaña, III, 140.
15. The Law is reproduced in *Méjico Revolucionario*, 18-30, and in Reyes, 125-32.
16. Reproduced in *Méjico Revolucionario*, 48-51.

17. Reproduced in *ibid.*, 52-9.
18. Sala, 49-50, 64-5; Rittenhouse, 249, 325-26, and Dromundo, 122.
19. Rittenhouse, 325; Magaña, II, 216-17.
20. Magaña, III, 268.
21. Díaz Soto y Gama, 159.
22. Magaña, V, 110.
23. Díaz Soto y Gama, 214-22. In these pages of his valuable work, the author presents information from the reports on their labors of several agronomists who headed agrarian commissions.
24. *Ibid.*, 224-26; Reyes, 97-8.
25. Díaz Soto y Gama, 224.
26. Reyes, 97-8; Díaz Soto y Gama, 267-69.
27. *Méjico Revolucionario*, 121, 142, 158-59, 172-73.
28. Reyes, 109.
29. *Ibid.*, 98; Sotelo Inclán, 203-04; Magaña, I, 39-40.

CHAPTER III

1. The Plan of San Luís is reproduced in *Documentos Históricos, Revolución y Regimen Maderista*, I, 69-76.
2. Magaña, II, 85.
3. *Ibid.*, IV, 203, 204, 206.
4. *Ibid.*, III, 252-57.
5. *Ibid.*, V, 17, 19-20.
6. Reyes, 135.
7. Magaña, III, 130-33.
8. *Ibid.*, I, 105-09.
9. *Ibid.*, I, 108-09, 138-39.
10. The Program is reproduced in *Méjico Revolucionario*, 37-47, and in *Fuentes*, I, 123-28.
11. Reproduced in *Méjico Revolucionario*, 31-37.
12. Magaña, V, 207-12, 218-26.
13. Reyes, 135-37.
14. Valverde, 174-75.
15. Reproduced in *Méjico Revolucionario*, 59-68.
16. Meléndez, I, 323.
17. Reproduced in *Méjico Revolucionario*, 68-72.
18. Reproduced in *Ibid.*, 74-80.
19. Reproduced in *Ibid.*, 80-4.
20. Reproduced in *ibid.*, 175-79.
21. "*Carranza engaña a los Obreros*," reproduced in *Méjico Revolucionario*, 180-82.

22. Reproduced in Dromundo, 179-84.
23, *Méjico Revolucionario*, 62.
24. Magaña, III, 252-57, and Dromundo, 90-5.
25. *Méjico Revolucionario*, 66.
26. *Ibid.*, 74-5.
27. *Ibid.*, 82.
28. *Ibid.*, 78.
29. *Fuentes,* I, 180.
30. Reyes, 106.
31. Meléndez, I, 323-24.
32. Reyes, 106.
33. *Ibid.*, 107-08.
34. Díaz Soto y Gama, 271. Also Meléndez, I, 323.

CHAPTER IV

1. Cline, 137. See also Bulnes, 164, and Vasconcelos, 452.
2. Dromundo, 82-3, 244.
3. Meléndez, I, 323.
4. Quirk, 8, 141-42, 154, 179, 223, 229-30, 269, *passim*.
5. Díaz Soto y Gama, 259.
6. Magaña, I, 14-5.
7. Meléndez, I, 320, 322, 355.
8. Dromundo, 146-49.
9. Meléndez, I, 372.
10. Dromundo, 169-71.
11. Quirk, 141, 136-43.
12. Dromundo, 102-03.
13. Obregón, 375, 399, 404-05, 410-11, 440.
14. Meléndez, I, 368, 371.
15. Basave del Castillo Negrete, IV, 51.
16. Magaña, V, 118-360; Ramírez Plancarte, 89-217.
17. Díaz Soto y Gama, 274.
18. Reyes, 146. The letter is reproduced in Reyes, 145-48, and in *Méjico Revolucionario*, 182-86. Also see Domingo, 44-5.
19. Magaña, III, 184-85. Quirk repeats this thesis, 230, 290-91, *passim*.
20. Fuentes, IV, 369-75.
21. Jenkins; *Fuentes,* I, xxxii-iii; Magaña, III, 184-85.
22. Martinez, 12-4, 4, 10, 8-9, 11, 6-7.
23. Silva Herzog, *Trayectoria Ideológica,* 41, 59.
24. Salazar, 147-49.
25. Díaz Soto y Gama, 203, 272-74.

26. *"La Revolución Política y la Revolución Campesina,"* reproduced in *Méjico Revolucionario,* 134-38.

27. Silva Herzog, *"La Revolución Mexicana,"* 30-1.

CHAPTER V

1. *Méjico Revolucionario,* 72.

2. Reproduced in *ibid.,* 72-4.

3. Meléndez, I, 374.

4. *Mejico Revolucionario,* 77. See also Zapata's Protest Before the Mexican People, May 1, 1917, in *ibid.,* 80-4, esp. 83-4.

5. *Ibid.,* 177.

6. Meléndez, I, 370; *Méjico Revolucionario,* 106, 168, *passim.*

7. Reyes, 147; *Méjico Revolucionario,* 184-85.

8. *"Obreros de la República i Salud!,"* reproduced in *Méjico Revolucionario,* 162-65,

9. Rittenhouse, 362. Translation by Rittenhouse, corrected by the author.

10. November 5, 1917; reproduced in *Méjico Revolucionario,* 119-26.

11. Magaña, II, 146.

12. Silva Herzog, *Trayectoria,* 104-05.

13. Salazar, 183, 217-23, 232-59; Silva Herzog, *Trayectoria,* 104-05, 123-24, 127-30.

14. *Fuentes,* I, 113-22.

15. Magaña, III, 197-225; Basave del Castillo Negrete, IV, 10-11; Gorrow, 60.

16. Tannenbaum (*Peace by Revolution,* 157) noted that it was Díaz Soto y Gama "who raised the issue of conflict between *Laborismo* and *Agrarianismo* in 1923, when the first national convention of labor and peasant groups met. The struggle for power between these groups has continued since." However, this was *zapatismo* without Zapata and, furthermore, the government encouraged conflict between the two groups to prevent their unification.

17. Breceda, II, 197-201.

18. Barragán Rodríguez, II, 36-8.

19. Palavicini, 245. For examples of Carranza's speeches, see those reproduced in *ibid.,* 243-60.

20. See Salazar, 124-32, 150-54, *passim.,* for an interpretation of the attitude of the *Casa del Obrero Mundial* toward the various revolutionary factions.

21. The decree and the law are reproduced in *Documentos Históricos,* I, 506-11, 517-22.

22. Silva Herzog, *Breve Historia*, II, 141, and Chevalier, 181-82.

23. For an indication of the significance to the Mexican people of Carranza's anti-imperialism, see Fabela, II, 111-23.

24. Silva Herzog, *Breve Historia*, II, 124-25, and *Trayectoria*, 65-6.

25. Tena Ramírez, 808-16, and Silva Herzog, *Breve Historia*, II, 253-54. Carranza's constitutional project and the Constitution of 1917 are reproduced in Tena Ramírez, 764-803, 817-81.

26. Taracena, 263.

27. Calero, 163-219, criticizes Carranza as a revolutionary and as a political leader from the point of view of an intelligent Mexican of conservative political inclinations. Calero contrasts Carranza's posture as a social revolutionary with his measures and policies as president.

28. *Ibid.*, 170-75, 189-90.

29. Chevalier, 182.

30. Salazar, 232-59.

31. *Ibid.*, 124.

32. See Gill, 299-305, for an account of the vicisitudes of Zapata's native village, Anenecuilco, Morelos, in its struggles from 1920 to the 1950s to obtain lands adequate for its needs.

LIST OF WORKS CITED

Barragán Rodríguez, Juan, *Historia del Ejército y de la Revolución Constitucionalista*. 2 vols. Mexico, 1946.

Basave del Castillo Negrete, Carlos, *Notas para la Historia de la Convención Revolucionaria, 1914-1915*. Papeles Historicos Mexicanos, vol. IV. Mexico, 1947.

Blanco Moheno, Roberto, *Crónica de la Revolución Mexicana*. 3 vols. Mexico, 1957-1961.

Breceda, Alfredo, *México Revolucionario, 1913-1917*. 2 vols. Madrid, 1920 and Mexico, 1941.

Bulnes, Francisco, *Los Grandes Problemas de México*. Mexico, 1926.

Calero, Manuel, *Un Decenio de Política Mexicana*. New York, 1920.

Chevalier, Francois, "Un Factor Decisivo de la Revolución Agraria de México: 'El Levantamiento de Zapata' (1911-1919)," *Cuadernos Americanos,* CXIII (Noviembre-Diciembre, 1960), 165-187.

Cline, Howard F., *The United States and Mexico*. Cambridge, Massachusetts, 1953.

Confidential Agency of the Provisional Government of Mexico, *The Soverign Revolutionary Convention of Mexico and the Attitude of General Francisco Villa*. Washington, D.C., 1915.

Cumberland, Charles Curtis, *Mexican Revolution; Genesis under Madero*. Austin, Texas, 1952.

Díaz Soto y Gama, Antonio, *La Revolución Agraria del Sur y Emiliano Zapata, su Caudillo*. Mexico, 1960.

Documentos Históricos de la Revolución Mexicana, *Revolución y Régimen Maderista*. vol. I. Mexico, 1964.

_____, *Revolución y Régimen Constitucionalista*. vol. I. Mexico, 1960.

Domingo, Alberto, "Vamos a 'Echarnos' a Zapata otra vez!," *Siempre!* Número 576 (Julio 8, 1964), 44-45.

Dromundo, Baltasar, *Emiliano Zapata*. Mexico, 1934.

Dunn, Harry H., *Zapata, The Crimson Jester of Mexico*. New York, 1934.

El Mundo. November 5, 1917. Habana, Cuba.

El Sur. January 1, 1918; March 15, 1918; April 20, 1918. Tlaltizapán, Morelos.

Fabela, Isidro, *Historia Diplomática de la Revolución Mexicana, 1912-1917*. 2 vols. Mexico, 1958-1959.

Fuentes para la Historia de la Revolución Mexicana, *Planes Políticos y otros Documentos*. vol. I. Mexico, 1954.

————, *Manifiestos Políticos, 1892-1912*. vol. IV. Mexico, 1957.

Gill, Mario, "Zapata: su Pueblo y sus Hijos," *Historia Mexicana*, II (Octubre-Diciembre, 1952), 294-312.

González-Blanco, Pedro, *De Porfirio Díaz a Carranza*. Madrid, 1916.

Gorrow, Bernard J., *The Mexican Social Upheaval of 1910: A Comparative Study of Theories of Revolutión*. Ph.D. Dissertation. University of Nebraska, 1951.

Gruening, Ernest, *Mexico and its Heritage*. New York, 1928.

Jenkins, Myra Ellen, *Ricardo Flores Magón and the Mexican Liberal Party*. Ph.D. Dissertation. University of New Mexico, 1953.

King, Rosa E., *Tempest Over Mexico*. Boston, 1938.

Link, Arthur S., *Wilson*. 5 vols. Princeton, New Jersey, 1947-1965.

Magaña, Gildardo (continued by Pérez Guerrero, Carlos), *Emiliano Zapata y El Agrarismo en México*. 5 vols. Mexico. 1951-1952.

Martínez, Paulino, *Causas de la Revolución en México y Como Efectuar la Paz; Bosquejo Sociológico*. Habana, 1914.

McBride, George McCutchen, *The Land Systems of México*. New York, 1923.

Méjico Revolucionario a los Pueblos de Europa y América, 1910-1918. Habana, n.d.

Meléndez, José T. ed., *Historia de la Revolucion Mexicana*. 2 vols. Mexico, 1936.

Obregón, Álvaro, *Ocho Mil Kilómetros en Campaña*. Mexico, 1917.

Palavicini, Felix F., ed., *El Primer Jefe*. Mexico, 1916.

————, *Grandes de México*. Mexico, 1948.

Parkes, Henry Bamford, *A History of Mexico*. 3rd ed. Boston, 1960.

Pinchon, Edgcumb, *Zapata the Unconquerable*. New York, 1941.

Quirk, Robert E. *The Mexican Revolution, 1914-1915; The Convention of Aguascalientes*. Bloomington, Indiana, 1960.

Ramírez Plancarte, Francisco, *La Cuidad de México durante la Revolución Constitucionalista*. 2nd ed. Mexico, 1941.

Reyes H., Alfonso, *Emiliano Zapata; Su Vida y su Obra*. Mexico, 1963.

Rittenhouse, Floyd, *Emiliano Zapata and the Suriano Rebellion: A Phase of the Agrarian Revolution in Mexico, 1910-1920*. Ph.D. Dissertation. Ohio State University, 1947.

Ross, Stanley R., *Francisco I. Madero, Apostle of Mexican Democracy,* New York, 1955.

Sala, Antenor, *Emiliano Zapata y El Problema Agrario en la República Mexicana.* Mexico, 1919.

Salazar, Rosendo, *La Casa del Obrero Mundial.* Mexico, 1962.

Silva Herzog, Jesús, *Breve Historia de la Revolución Mexicana.* 2 vols. Mexico, 1960.

————, *Trayectoria Ideológica de la Revolución Mexicana.* Mexico, 1963.

————, "La Revolución Mexicana," *Siempre!,* Numero 612 (Marzo 17, 1965), 30-31.

Simpson, Eyler N., *The Ejido; Mexico's Way Out.* Chapel Hill, North Carolina, 1937.

Sotelo Inclán, Jesus, *Raíz y Razón de Zapata.* Mexico, 1943.

Tannenbaum, Frank, *The Mexican Agrarian Revolution.* New Yrok, 1929.

————, *Peace by Revolution.* New York, 1933.

Taracena, Alfonso, *En el Vértigo de la Revolución Mexicana.* Mexico, 1930.

————, *La Tragedia Zapatista.* Mexico, 1931.

————, *Mi Vida en el Vértigo de la Revolución Mexicana.* Mexico, 1936.

————, *Venustiano Carranza.* Mexico, 1963.

Tena Ramírez, Felipe, *Leyes Fundamentales de México, 1808-1964.* 2nd rev. ed. Mexico, 1964.

Urquizo, Francisco L., *Don Venustiano Carranza; El Hombre; el Político; el Caudillo.* 2nd ed. Mexico, 1939.

————, *Carranza; El Hombre, el Político, el Caudillo, el Patriota.* Mexico, 1957.

Urrea, Lic. Blas (pseud. for Luís Cabrera), *Veinte Años Después.* Mexico, 1937.

Valverde, Sergio, *Apuntes para la Historia de la Revolucíon y de la Política en el Estado de Morelos.* Mexico, 1933.

Vasconcelos, José, *Breve Historia de México.* Mexico, 1956.

INDEX

AGUASCALIENTES, 22
Aguascalientes Convention (1914),
26, 44, 71, 93, 120, 134, 136*f*
Amezcua, Jenaro, 54, 94*ff*, 105,
107
Anarchism, 97
Anenecuilco, 13
Ángeles, Felipe, 16, 19, 32
Anti-religious campaign, 72
Apizaco, 90
Arriaga, Camilo, 63
Ayala, Plan of, 5, 16, 25*ff*, 40*ff*,
53, 59*ff*, 72, 74, 79, 85*ff*, 93*f*,
115, 117, 120, 125, 136*ff*; ratifi-
cation, 42, 60; relation to Plan of
San Luis, 13, 17, 40*f*, 59*ff*, 70,
72, 115

BARRÁGAN   RODRÍGUEZ,
JUAN, 136
Blanco, Lucio, 22
Blanco Moheno, Roberto, 137
Bolsheviks, 112
Bourgeois democracy, 63
Breceda, Alfredo, 24, 133
Bucareli agreements, 125

CABRERA, LUÍS, 18, 32, 117,
135
Calderón, Esteban B., 118
Caja Rural de Préstamos (agri-
cultural credit bank), 53
Cal y Mayor, Rafael, 89
Calles, Plutarco Elías, 124, 126,
130
Cananea, 106
Cárdenas, Lázaro, 41, 55, 58, 110,
124, 126, 128, 130

Carrancistas, agrarian reform, 21,
25, 49, 155*ff*; anti-imperialist
policy, 117; conflict with Villa
and Zapata 22*ff*; labor policy,
75*f*, 116; political program, 24;
social reforms, 119
Carranza, Venustiano, 20, 23*ff*,
32, 37, 42, 45, 54, 70, 74, 75,
85*f*, 92, 104*f*, 115, 118*f*, 120*ff*,
133*ff*
Casa del Obrero Mundial, 72, 98,
106*f*, 112, 116, 121
Casals, Prudencio, 35
Caudillismo, 113*f*
Cautla, 30*f*
Celaya, 29, 90*f*
Chiapas, 84, 89, 109
Chietla, 91
Chevalier, Francois, 85
Chihuahua, 22, 29, 52, 88, 109
Chilpancingo, 20
Chinameca, 36
Cholula, 91
Ciudad Juárez, 14
Ciudad Juárez, Treaties of, 14, 17
Cline, Howard, 83
Coahuila, 88, 90
Coatetelco, 52*n*
Cocoyac, 52*n*
*Confederación Regional de Obre-
ros Mexicanos* (CROM), 121
Constituent Convention of 1916-
17, 45, 127, 133
Constitution of 1857, 59, 118, 133
Constitution of 1917, 69, 119;
agrarian reform (Article 27), 49;
labor policy (Article 123), 76;
129, municipal reform (Article